Write the Word

WRITE THE WORD

A Creative Writing Text

by William Folprecht

Illustrated by Ed Parker

mott media BOX 236, MILFORD, MICHIGAN 48042

EVANGELICAL CHRISTIAN PUBLISHERS ASSOCIATION ecpa MEMBER

LIBRARY OF CONGRESS CATALOGING IN PUBLICATION DATA

Folprecht, William, 1912-
Write the word!

Includes index.

SUMMARY: A guide for the beginning author including information on marketing, writers' clubs and conferences, and agents and offering advice about word awareness, vocabulary development, finding ideas, and submitting manuscripts.

1. Authorship—Handbooks, manuals, etc. [1. Authorship] I. Parker, Ed. II. Title.

PN147.F58 808'.042 76-18091

ISBN 0-915134-15-2

This book is dedicated to the memory of
Clara Folprecht
a Christian mother who always encouraged
my efforts for Christ

A Note to Teachers

This book may not read like the usual classroom textbook, for it tells informally of lessons learned in editing, writing, and teaching over a span of some twenty-five years.

Since the goal of ultimate publication is paramount in the book, a word or two concerning this objective is in order. Usually high school students are serving their apprenticeship at learning writing skills, but young or old, the expectation of seeing one's material published is exciting and joyous. This incentive, I hope, will encourage your students to want very much to learn more about all aspects of the writing profession.

I hope and pray that sending forth this volume will inspire, challenge and assist young Christians (and their teachers) to write better and more often—that they might help glorify our Lord and help bring in His kingdom.

In His Name
William Folprecht

Psalm 8.

Contents

Introduction to Students

This workbook combines three basics
for all young authors:
1. Inspiration 2. Information 3. Instruction

Inspiration. All beginning writers, regardless of background, often become discouraged and need occasional lifting of their spirits. Throughout this volume I have tried to give you this "pat on the back." As an editor I tried always to take the sting out of rejection slips by writing a simple line or two of personal advice. When I left the editorial desk, writers sent me letters of appreciation. Words of encouragement, I hope, you will find in these pages.

Information. Young writers are unfamiliar with marketing details, editors' needs, the process of transferring a typed manuscript to the printed page. I shall try to share my experiences as an author who has had published over 400 stories and articles. My "trials and joys" as a juvenile editor are reflected here, too.

Instruction. I am convinced that while there is no "royal road" to learning to write successfully, there is a method to learning how to write creatively and effectively. A study of the art of writing does not automatically lead to the development of a Hemingway or Faulkner, but an experienced (or at least an older) author can share his tribulations and triumphs with budding writers.

A final word: Be alert to capture and hold on to any new ideas that occur to you while reading this book. Catch those fleeting thoughts and write them down! They will come only to you, in their own peculiar way, and they can be valuable. They may result in—who knows?—fortune, fame, an inner satisfaction indescribable except to a real writer.

P.S. Do read in full all the Bible verses mentioned.
The Scriptures are inspiring. They lead us to Jesus Christ our Savior, help strengthen our faith, guide us in the Christian life, and challenge us daily to seek and to do God's will.

Chapter 1

The Writer

"In the beginning God created
the heaven and the earth" *(Genesis 1:1)*.

Man reaches his highest development when he is creative. When he spans waterways with strong cables and builds bridges, when he reaches into the blue with giant skyscrapers, when he builds great dams to supply power or to irrigate parched lands, he is akin to the Master Creator, God.

Not all of us can build bridges, erect tall buildings, dam up bodies of water. Not all of us are cut out to be engineers, architects, mathematicians.

Yet every person has some creative talent. And for some, it is the creative use of words, the assembling of the letters of the alphabet in such a way that others are amused, entertained, instructed, inspired, helped.

The field of creative writing is a vast one, open to all who desire to communicate ideas, hopes and aspirations, to open up new avenues of thought via the printed page. The creative writer is engaged in an effort linking him with the immortals of literature.

When you, as a student-writer begin to create, you sit in the grand company of men and women like John Milton, William Shakespeare, Nathaniel Hawthorne, Pearl Buck, Kenneth Roberts, Jane Austen, John Bunyan, Henry David Thoreau, and hundreds of other writers who have brought joy, hope, humor or satisfaction to millions of readers.

One fact often forgotten is that these authors had to go

through an apprenticeship. They had to write and rewrite, to develop facility with the written word.

Therefore, don't be afraid to play in the "minor leagues" for a season or so. Stan Musial, Mickey Mantle, Sandy Koufax, Willie Mays, and other baseball stars all put in their time in the minors. That's where they gained experience, where the rough edges were sandpapered off, where they learned the "know-how" that later brought in, in some instances, the fabulous salaries earned in the majors.

In some cases, athletes who later turned out to be the All-Stars of the baseball world played on sandlots, or on high school or college teams. Here they weren't paid for their efforts, but they picked up techniques, studied the game, matured in their sport. Not one of them would deny the value of those early years.

To learn how to play successfully, some athletes have gone to unusual lengths. Andy Bathgate, long a hockey great with the New York Rangers, used to play hockey in Canada at five each morning because that was the only hour a rink two miles away was available for him and his teammates. Later, skating before thousands in Madison Square Garden, he capitalized on the experience gained at those inconvenient, early morning games.

Smaller papers and magazines that may publish your material can give you your "sandlot" and "minor league" experience as a writer.

If your school has a newspaper, write for it. Don't be discouraged if at first your articles are not published. Keep writing them. I sold one of my articles on its seventeenth submission to a national magazine! Have faith in yourself.

Or your school may have a "Pen and Ink" mimeographed magazine, as our school has. Write a short story, poem, or article for it.

Submit material to your local newspaper. In our area, one girl has a weekly column of high school social activities in the paper. In another weekly, a high school boy covers local school sports. Both have "by-lines." The editors feel their material worthy of regular publication.

Perhaps your church has a newspaper, or your youth society. Submit articles. Get in the habit of writing regularly, trying to get your material in print, somewhere.

The first paragraph I ever had published appeared years ago in my local church's newspaper. It was a brief item about a hike our Sunday School class took. Yes, I still have it. It was the first of many, many paragraphs to be printed. Only paragraphs, but they were a beginning. Remember the words of the Eastern sage: "The journey of ten thousand miles begins with the taking of the first step."

If you are reading these words, you have already embarked upon such a journey, one on which you may meet people you might never have met, have experiences that might never have occurred.

Don't be ashamed of small successes. My first check years ago was for the huge sum of $3.50. When I showed it to my mother, she simply said: "Well, you have to crawl before you walk! Keep it up!" And I did, with the checks continuing to come in. And growing larger.

Writers must have tough skins. Like an athlete, you have to be able to take it. Don't be discouraged if your early efforts are rejected. Kenneth Roberts, in his book *I Wanted to Write,* says that Booth Tarkington's early stories were returned so fast he thought the envelopes were made of rubber! Paul Gallico, former sports editor of a New York daily, a successful playwright and free lance novelist, revealed in an article that even well-known writers occasionally receive rejection slips.

Sometimes the successful author is simply the writer

who has the persistence to keep at the long grind. Like a cross-country runner, it's not the speed, but the endurance that counts.

Besides endurance, a writer needs words and ideas. We must assume a fundamental knowledge of grammar, too, though even successful authors must delve again and again into a handbook or grammar to verify certain rules. Grammar is important, but this book will not cover that familiar ground in detail.

Keep a pencil handy when reading this volume. When something strikes you, write it down on the lines at the close of this chapter, or in a notebook, if this book will not be yours permanently.

If you are serious about becoming a writer, always read with a pencil at hand. In our living room there are three tables, each with a lamp and pencil at all times. Whenever I am reading a newspaper, book, magazine, yes, even bills, pencil and paper are handy.

When I read a book, I use a folded sheet of paper as a bookmark. You can do the same, jotting on it anything that occurs to you as worth pursuing for an article or a short story. Write down your thoughts, always precious to a writer, for they don't always come when you expect them. Seize them at the moment they do, and keep them together in one notebook.

I cannot stress enough the necessity of capturing ideas. Years ago I had read an article in a writer's magazine and going to sleep that night, was mulling it over. The author had suggested that if you wrote a certain type of short story, try another area for a change of pace.

I had been writing strictly sports and adventure stories for boys. I suddenly got the idea to write a comical sports story. But what?

Basketball had been my particular sport. How about a funny basketball story? That idea, coming at that late hour, I hurriedly arose to jot down. It resulted in a 2,500 word story, "Basketball Blimp." I sold it to a youth weekly, *Vision*.

At a school function, I felt very warm. I asked myself where might it be warmer! I thought of the jungles, and made a note to write a jungle story.

Ideas come at all odd times, usually when you're not even looking for them.

Reading the *New York Times* one day, I noted a single paragraph about some men climbing a mountain. It inspired me to write "Mountain Peril," which *Upward*, another youth periodical, published. I remember tearing out the little paragraph as well as making a note about writing a mountain tale.

Be alert for such ideas. Develop the habit of taking notes. Don't worry about how sketchy they may be, just get them down.

Notes which you may have taken down while reading this chapter might read like this:

Don't be afraid to play in the minors!
Don't be discouraged!
Try to get your material published.
Be alert for new ideas.
The habits of the owl.

Now, how did that last one get on the list? I've inserted it as an example of the kind of idea that may occur to imaginative people, that may seem entirely unrelated to what they are reading or hearing. It might be an idea for an article which struck you while I was writing of something else. The point is, get it down. It's *your* idea. If you are interested enough, you might do some research and come up with a good piece.

Don't let the butterflies fly away. Catch those new ideas and write them down! A clearly written thought is worth a thousand ambiguous, fuzzy ones tucked away in your mental attic.

Read all kinds of material. Read to develop your mind, to widen your intellectual horizon, to become a better person. A writer utilizes all of himself. A book read a decade before may unconsciously influence writing. Something heard at a lecture years ago might be included in an article.

Read novels, plays, essays, poetry, anything you come across. Read humorous and serious pieces, deep and superficial works. Read to be entertained and to be instructed. Read to be challenged and encouraged.

Read biographies, particularly of authors. They lived their lives in a different time and clime, perhaps, but you can still benefit from reading about the trials and victories of other writers.

Read for the development of your own writing skills. Read the periodicals for budding and experienced authors, such as *The Writer,* or *The Writer's Digest.* Send for sample copies if your school doesn't subscribe. Or perhaps your school will, if you explain their value to your librarian.

Discipline yourself to write regularly. Make yourself turn out so much copy each week or each day. One teacher declared that the longest road in the world is from the easy chair to the writing desk. Tear yourself away from the television set, or whatever tends to keep you from turning out material.

Be tough with yourself. I set a goal of 25 stories and articles each summer, when school is over, and I do my best to turn them out, one year ending with 27. Set goals. Say to yourself, "I'll write 500 words before I grab that snack," or "I'll write 750 words before I turn on the TV." Don't give in to temptation. Force yourself to do the work you set out to do.

For awhile, to turn out copy regularly may be tough. That's where a course in school helps, a course where you must complete assignments. För some, this is the best way to get in the habit of turning out material regularly.

Writing is a lonely job, so many writers join writer's clubs, attend seminars, lectures, summer conferences, take special courses. The writer must not become a recluse. He needs the inspiration and encouragement of his fellows.

A writing class not only forces you to turn out assignments, it also gives you the fellowship of like-minded people—which helps to create "esprit de corps."

Lonely it may be, but writing brings many compensations. One is your creation of something not in the world before. You have turned out a short story, a poem, an essay, an article. The feeling of accomplishment cannot be evaluated. Money cannot measure it.

Such inner satisfaction reminds me of an anonymous piece of writing I ran across decades ago:

> No endeavor is in vain,
> Its reward is in the doing,
> And the rapture of pursuing
> Is the prize the victors gain.

The joy of writing, of knowing one has done his best to create something new, this is a happiness only true composers of music, word or brush can feel.

And now, you have been reading for some time. How about tackling your first writing assignment? After all, this is a book on writing, and the only proven way to master the art is to write.

Select one of the following quotations and write a 300-400 word composition on it, for grading and analysis by your instructor.

"Time ripens all things; no man is born wise."
(Cervantes)

"One today is worth two tomorrows."
(Benjamin Franklin)

"By and by is easily said."
(Hamlet, William Shakespeare)

"Thank God every morning when you get up that you have something to do that day which must be done, whether you like it or not."
(Anonymous)

Let's talk for a while now about your reasons for writing. Why do you want to be a writer? What do you expect to gain from placing words on paper? Do you feel a driving necessity to write, or do you have other reasons for writing?

In the courses I have conducted over the past years, my students have offered several motives. Perhaps yours is one of them.

(1) *Fame.* Some of my students have declared that they hoped to become well-known as a result of their writing, perhaps not as famous as a Dickens or a Saroyan, but at least recognizable as an average author whose works are reviewed in the Sunday papers.

(2) *Money.* Some have said they hoped to make money. In fact, one student had already received a check for writing a letter to a newspaper, a letter which had been judged the best of the teen-age epistles received that week. The money whetted her appetite for more. This, too, is a reasonable goal.

(3) *Inspiration.* Some were interested in helping others. They felt that just as they had in turn been helped by reading a story or an article, they, too, might inspire a reader to live a happier life. By reading of problems solved in short stories and novels, we, too, are helped when it comes to making decisions that may affect our personal lives.

(4) *Catharsis.* Several students advised that they "just had to get it out of them." And writing does just that. It reminds us of a story about Abraham Lincoln.

A friend, vehement, angry, told Lincoln that someone had done him great harm and he intended to retaliate. Lincoln advised him to write a stiff note to the other party,

telling him what he thought of him. "Make it as strong as possible," the President urged. "Give him both barrels."

Then he paused. "But don't send the letter. Put it in your desk for a week."

Lincoln knew that by letting off steam, the friend would feel better. He also knew that after a week, he might think better of sending the letter, too. But the point is that he would "get it out of his system."

Some time ago I met a writer at the world-famous Chautauqua Institution, at a summer resort where writers, artists, and musicians gathered. He had written several books, and had made quite a fortune.

Yet he told me that on occasion he would dash off small pieces for paltry sums, just because he had "to get the thing off his chest."

(5) *Self-satisfaction.* In a way this is related to the previous desire to write, yet it has a different aspect. Some writers simply like to see their material in print. Even after I have spent the check which I received for an article or story, when I see the piece in black and white, with my byline, I feel an even greater thrill.

(6) *????????????* Do you have another reason for writing? One of my personal aims is to "write the word" of my Christian experience. Add others to the list, and write to me, in care of the publisher. I'd like to hear about it. And I know my students would, too.

Here, then, are reasons why people write. They seek fame, money, to be helpful, to get it out of their system, and simply, self-satisfaction.

Note that many people do not write only for money. Samuel Johnson is said to have declaimed, "No man, unless he was a blockhead, ever wrote except for money." Now Johnson was a wise man, and a good writer, but he appears to have been in error in this regard.

Most people appreciate money for their writing. But I have met many, such as students in my writing classes, who have not thought much about it. I have personally known many who have written for magazines for reasons other than financial: preachers, teachers, physicians, lawyers, and others.

Many people take pains to express themselves in letters to friends and relatives with no thought of monetary return. In fact, my wife and I have been chuckling over a lengthy letter written us by our son.

No, he isn't writing for money. He is a counselor in a church summer camp, and he has just written of his three day orientation session. It has amused us no end to hear his teen-age description of some of the activities, including a farcical softball game between the boy and girl counselors.

My son wrote, as many of us do, simply to communicate, to tell us what's going on.

Even with such noble and practical motives, writing can often be a disillusioning vocation. There are times when it doesn't seem worth the candle, a useless chore. That's the time to turn to your "rainy day" mottoes. Like the one suggested earlier, "No man is born wise." I have never yet heard of a writer who was produced full-blown, an instant professional. All of them served some sort of apprenticeship.

William Heuman, magazine and television writer, began by writing for religious weeklies, then for the "pulps" and later for the better-paying "slicks."

During apprenticeship, the young writer needs a lot of encouragement. This is when the comments of successful authors and others, detailing their own, personal disappointments, "buck up" the young author. So read about the early lives of authors, and learn how discouraged they might have been and how they finally triumphed. Like Elijah in I Kings 19:4-18.

Develop the habit of reading a book of quotations oc-

casionally. Some of the old tried-and-true statements really strengthen one's resolve to continue.

> King Hassan, well beloved, was wont to say,
> When aught went wrong, or any project failed:
> "Tomorrow, friends, will be another day!"
> And in that faith he slept and so prevailed.
>
> *("Tomorrow," James Buckham)*

One of the greatest personalities I ever met was Dr. Edgar DeWitt Jones, former president of the Federal Council of Churches of Christ in America (now the National Council of Churches). Although he studied to be a lawyer, he became a preacher. Eloquent, challenging, a giant of a man physically and spiritually, he was in great demand all over the United States.

A Lincoln scholar, he was considered one of the authorities on the life of the Great Emancipator. His large volume on the lives of the world's greatest preachers who appeared at the famous Beecher Lectures each year at Yale University *(The Royalty of the Pulpit)* is a monumental work for all clergymen.

It was my privilege to spend several days at different times with this writer-lawyer-preacher. And I shall never forget his emphasis upon what others, too, have declared to be the secret of a writer's success.

"Get the idea," he told me, "then brood upon it, and then persist until it has been successfully spread abroad."

Get the idea, then brood upon it, and then write and try to publish it.

For my "brooding," I have a manila folder into which I toss all kinds of ideas, clippings, anything that suggests an idea. During the school year, they remain in that folder. When school is out, and my time is my own, I open the folder to see what has happened to my ideas.

I have written upon its cover the words: "Germinating Seeds." That is just what the folder contains—the seeds of ideas. If I were to try to write about them immediately, they might not produce much harvest. But lying in my subconscious, the ideas have been growing, developing almost untouched, except that I do occasionally riffle through the notes during the school year when I toss in new pieces.

Such brooding helps to mature thoughts, make them more usable when you are ready to write them out. This folder idea, or a notebook, is insurance against the rainy day when one looks for ideas to write about.

The work habits of writers vary as much as their personalities. You may prefer to be very methodical, perhaps using 3 x 5 cards for ideas you collect. That's up to you. Writers utilize all sorts of devices to get them going.

One great author was asked what was his inspiration. He said his wife usually told him some new piece of furniture was needed or the rug was wearing thin.

All writers have their own methods. Some writers have distinct idiosyncracies. Hemingway couldn't use a typewriter, according to one source, but stood up to write by hand. A successful writer and editor, Guy P. Leavitt, of the Standard Publishing Company in Cincinnati, told me, "I can't think unless I'm sitting with my fingers on the keys of a typewriter."

In general, I would suggest that you learn to type. A one-semester course in school will do it, or learn on your own. Any script submitted for publication to any reputable publishing house must be typed. Even our school newspaper demands it.

In connection with your writing habits, steel yourself against interruptions. They will come—don't worry about that!—but learn to take them philosophically.

Never leave your writing at the end of a complete sentence to answer the door, the phone, or to go in to eat dinner. Stop in the middle of the sentence, let it dangle. When you return, you will find that by reading the first half of that sentence, you will be able to pick up the thread of your thinking and go on. If you end the sentence, or the thought, neatly, clipping it off at the end of the sentence, an iron curtain seems to descend. Try it and see.

Try always to write the best you can, even with first drafts, though you know you will be revising. Make it the best you can first off.

And yet—don't sit and waste half an hour because you are stuck for a word. You can always search out a better word by means of a thesaurus or dictionary later. Keep writing!

Make time for your writing. Each of us has only twenty-four hours in the day. We have to sleep, eat, perform other chores vital to life. But somewhere in the day, there is that hour, or maybe two, when you can, by forfeiting some other leisure time activity, sit down and write.

Fasten upon that time, and resolve to use it.

Obtain a good dictionary and use it. This is so elementary that I blush to mention it, but even basic advice needs repeating. The dictionary habit is one all authors *must* cultivate. It's like the surgeon constantly exercising his fingers.

Dr. John Ruskin Dallas, physician and surgeon, played the accordian, both to try to relax from his tension-filled work at the hospital and to make his fingers as flexible as possible for the operating room.

The writer must have a suppleness of mind just as the surgeon must have a suppleness of fingers. He must have words at his instant command.

One of the questions young authors ask is whether or not they should discuss stories or articles they are considering. This is an important question. What should you do when you have an idea for a story or essay?

Most authors advise that not to discuss projected works is best. "Don't talk about it!" they urge. "Write about it!"

There are exceptions to this rule. Often a writer will meet with an editor, and mention two or three ideas for articles. Sometimes this is good. Many writers submit inquiry letters to editors, suggesting ideas for articles.

But for fiction, discussing a story you have in mind, say, about a man scuba diving in the waters of the Gulf of Mexico, is senseless. *Write* the story and let all of your emotion, all of your telling skill come out in the writing. Far too often, when you tell someone about your plot, you get satisfaction from the person's reaction, and that is enough to put off the actual writing. It also takes the keenness off the telling.

You want to be a writer, not an orator or lecturer, although you might have talent along those lines, too. Primarily you are writing, conveying information, sensation by the written word. Concentrate on that alone.

What should you do when your compositions do not receive good grades, when there is little to encourage you to continue? Keep on, anyway. Consider it all part of the game. Remember, every piece you write brings you that much closer to recognition and reward. Keep putting your thoughts down.

Three class projects your group might incorporate to brighten class sessions and add interest in creative writing:

1. Write a class story and have it mimeographed

or reproduced on the ditto machine for class distribution. Here's the way our class handled it: Have a class discussion to vote upon the names of the two major characters, a fellow and a girl, and the opening locale or background of the story. One of ours was set on a beach, where a girl, Lisa, met a boy named Eric. That's all the class decided upon. Each day the paper was passed to another student who added a paragraph or two. When the last student had written the final part, the story was given to a student to type the ditto master.

Before we wrote the story, we read one written by the previous class.

2. Have a guest lecturer, someone who has had a great deal of material published. This might be the town historian, a teacher, a newspaper man or an author living in the community. It's amazing the number of people who are happy to address a class. Our school has a "Living Resource" file listing various speakers.

3. Present regularly, once or twice a week, student summaries of either articles in *The Writer* magazine or parts of writers' biographies that will inspire the class. Someone has said that while writing cannot perhaps be taught, it can be learned by the contagious enthusiasm of a class. Use your class, then, as a workshop or seminar, where you all share experiences in the writing game.

Write a 300-400 word composition on:

"Why I Want to Write"
or "The Rewards of Writing"
or "Good Habits for Writers"

Write on the lines below any ideas for future writing which have occurred to you while reading this chapter:

Chapter 2

The Writer's Tools: Words

"It was needful for me to write unto you that ye should earnestly contend for the faith" *(Jude 3)*.

If you were a carpenter, you would need certain tools to build a house: saws, chisels, planes, hammers, and other equipment. You couldn't work without them.

To be a writer, you must possess tools, too, and know how to use them. Your tools are the words you place on paper to build your "house," your story or article. And the more tools you have, the better equipped you are to do the job.

If a carpenter has to stop work every once in a while because he doesn't have a screwdriver, or a saw, or a drill, he'll fall behind on the job. Likewise, an author has to have an adequate storehouse of his tools—words—and they must be at his side for instant use.

This chapter will discuss three ways to develop vocabulary.

One of the most enjoyable is simply to read a great deal. Since reading for most of us is a joy, not a chore, this is a boon. It is somewhat like getting a job as a lifeguard. You're crazy about the water in the first place, and you're getting paid to sit on the beach. What more could you ask for?

If you are interested in developing your writing skills, you are already interested in words, and you are a born reader, as most writers are. So as you read, whatever it may be—the Bible, a story, a poem, a report, the newspaper—you are unconsciously adding certain words to your vocabulary. You can add to your knowledge of words even more by reading more carefully.

We have said that you should always read with a pencil and paper handy, for new ideas that may occur while reading some other writer's ideas. We also suggest that you write down words which fascinate you. Maybe you don't have the time or the opportunity to get to a dictionary at that moment. Nevertheless, you have "captured" the word and after a while, can look it up.

Make it part of your own vocabulary in one of several ways.

Read the dictionary entry, noting derivation and the word's several meanings. Some authors like to look it up in a thesaurus, a dictionary of synonyms, as well. Others like to use it in a sentence of their own, either aloud, to themselves, or in written form. You may even want to practice writing sentences using the word.

Or you may want to add it to your small looseleaf notebook, to see how many new words you can acquire within a given time.

But read with discernment, adding to your stock interesting words. Be on the *qui vive* to grab new words as they come along. They may have been in use for hundreds of years, but they are new to you. Don't be concerned only with words which have recently entered our language, such as isotope, telemetry, or sonar.

Learn the words in use for years, understood by men and women everywhere. Jesus spoke so clearly that "the common people heard him gladly" (Mark 12:37). Later you may take a course in semantics, the study of the history of words, and you may learn far more than you ever dreamed possible about the sounds and symbols we use to communicate with each other.

For the present, confine yourself to looking up each word new to you as it comes along. Don't be lazy about it.

Write it down. Don't say, "I'll remember to look it up." Don't trust memory. When you write it down, chances are you will really search out its meaning, but if you trust yourself to remember to do so, you probably won't.

Get into the writing-it-down-and-looking-it-up habit. It pays off.

We have suggested that extensive reading will widen your vocabulary horizon. That is true. You want more words to be able to express yourself more effectively. But in your reading you are interested, too, in the proper use of those words, not just in learning their meaning.

You want to have the tools, but you want to be able to use them. Like a mechanic working on a car, you must have the right tools and know how to use them.

Note how an author utilizes his words.

Note, for example, someone like Edgar Allan Poe, the master of the eerie, suspense tale. See how he builds up a mental picture.

Here, for example, is a selection from his short story, "A Tale of the Ragged Mountains":

> I found myself at the foot of a high mountain, and looking down into a vast plain, through which wound a majestic river. On the margin of this river stood an Eastern-looking city, such as we read of in the Arabian Tales, but of a character even more singular than any there described.
>
> From my position, which was far above the level of the town, I could perceive its every nook and corner, as if delineated on a map. The streets seemed innumerable, and crossed each other irregularly in all directions, but were rather long winding alleys than streets, and absolutely swarmed with inhabitants.
>
> The houses were wildly picturesque. On every hand was a wilderness of balconies, of verandas, of minarets, of shrines, and fantastically carved oriels. Bazaars abounded; and there were displayed rich

> wares in infinite variety and profusion—silks, muslins, the most dazzling cutlery, the most magnificent jewels and gems.
>
> Besides these things, were seen, on all sides, banners and palanquins, litters with stately dames close-veiled, elephants gorgeously caparisoned, idols grotesquely hewn, drums, banners, and gongs, spears, silver and gilden maces. And amid the crowd, and the clamor, and the general intricacy and confusion, - amid the million of black and yellow men, turbaned and robed, and of flowing beard, there roamed a countless multitude of holy filleted bulls, while vast legions of the filthy but sacred ape clambered, chattering and shrieking, about the cornices of the mosques, or clung to the minarets and oriels.

Herman Melville is worth studying to see how an author uses his tools. Take a passage from *Moby Dick:*

> Reality outran apprehension; Captain Ahab stood upon his quarter-deck.
>
> There seemed no sign of common bodily illness about him, nor of the recovery from any. . . . His whole high, broad form seemed made of solid bronze, and shaped in an unalterable mold, like Cellini's cast Perseus. Threading its way out from among his gray hairs, and continuing right down one side of his tawny scorched face and neck, till it disappeared in his clothing, you saw a slender, rodlike mark, lividly whitish. It resembled that perpendicular seam sometimes made in the straight, lofty trunk of a great tree, when the upper lightning tearingly darts down it, and without wrenching a single twig, peels and grooves out the bark from top to bottom ere running off into the soil, leaving the tree still greenly alive, but branded. Whether that mark was born with him, or whether it was the scar left by some desperate wound, no one could certainly say. By some tacit

consent, throughout the voyage little or no allusion was made to it, especially by the mates.

Studying the great writers of the past provides know-how for writers-in-training.

If you were to stand beside a master artisan and watch him work, you would study how he achieved a certain effect. Diligent appraisal of the work of successful authors also teaches.

Now skilled professionals in all fields once stood on the sidelines and watched the masters perform. It is part of the story of human endeavor. Those now experienced, the old "pros," began as rank amateurs, hoping and praying one day to be as good as the men and women they looked up to.

Learn from the masters. See how they used words to get across their ideas.

Never try simply to emulate them when you write, for they wrote in their own way. You must write in your own way, but study theirs.

The lengthy paragraphs of Dickens and Melville are not for today's literary world. Today we write in a somewhat journalistic style. The modern reader doesn't expect to have to wade through long, descriptive passages of scenes laid out for him. With a few, deft strokes today's writer paints a vivid picture. During the action, characterization and background are sketched in.

Even though it sounds paradoxical, study the authors, but don't copy them.

In addition to reading and analyzing the works of others to add to your toolchest, resolve deliberately to develop vocabulary. In talking with the members of our classes from year to year, we have found that there are several interesting ways to build a bigger supply of tools or words.

Some students averred that they are great crossword puzzle addicts. Some will say there are far too many unusual words in such puzzles. Still, if you like doing them, try to solve them. After all, they do make you think, which is part of writing. If along the way you pick up additions to your vocabulary, it's all worthwhile.

Every good writer will study the make-up, the background of words. A knowledge of prefixes, suffixes, and roots will enlarge his storehouse. When he learns the meaning of the prefix "bene" (well, good), he then knows the meaning of such words as benevolent, benign, benefactor, beneficiary.

The knowledge of such suffixes as "ette" (small, little) helps him understand the meaning of kitchenette, novelette, marionette.

A serious grasp of the roots of many of our words will help most. If "teleos" means "from afar" and "graph" or "gram" means "write," you can figure out the meaning of "telegram"—a writing from afar. Television—pictures or images from afar, telephone—distant sounds or voices, and a host of other associations suggest themselves.

When we learn that "phobia" means "fear," everytime we see a word with these letters in it, we are on the alert to discover the aversion mentioned.

So take the time to study families of words, or roots, suffixes, and prefixes.

One of the methods some of our classes use is to add five new words each day to the list in a notebook. These words are sometimes given to the class by the teacher from an approved list.

Students can bring in words from reading newspapers, magazines, books or class anthology. Wherever they come from, such words make excellent additions to any student or writer's collection.

But don't gorge yourself. We usually eat 21 meals each week. We don't eat them all in one day. We spread them out.

The same applies to words. If you try to absorb too many at any one time, you'll suffer "intellectual indigestion." It is far better to add a few words regularly than to try to gulp down large amounts at one time.

I remember a student who came to me to say that at first he had rebelled against the idea of putting five new words in his notebook each day, Monday through Friday. Then he had begun to think about it.

"That's eight hundred each year for the four years of high school," he told me. "That makes 3,200 new words. Suppose I add that many in college. I'll have added 6,400 new words, plus the other new words I pick up by myself along the way."

He stood looking at me. "I never realized just how much I could add to my vocabulary by just adding five new words a day five days a week."

As you keep at gaining words, take it easy. As Isaiah wrote: "here a little, and there a little" (Isa. 28:10). Stay with it. Develop a self-discipline that makes you eager to keep building vocabulary.

On the market at the moment are inexpensive paperbacks containing a variety of ways to develop vocabulary. Following some of these methods cannot help but increase your depository of words.

Reader's Digest publishes a list of twenty words each month. True, some of them are "tricky," but the opportunity to add some of them to your own storehouse is worth the effort of testing your word-power. As a budding author, you should be eager to grasp any such group of

words, see how many you already know, and then add the ones you don't.

Although there are some who contend that word-games on television are a waste of a viewer's time, such diversions can "put you on your toes." They usually feature the use of synonyms, of immense help to a writer. Certainly the person interested in words will find such shows of greater value than old movies, song-and-dance variety shows, and similar programs offering little mental stimulus.

Speaking of games, some of the members of our classes have advocated the playing of word games such as Scrabble, in which the accent is on building words. There is entertainment value, too, in such a pastime. If the writer has time to play such games, they provide further opportunities to focus upon word tools.

In adding to your vocabulary remember that the slang of today often is gone tomorrow. Phrases which now might be in popular use among teenagers, college youth, sports fans, and others, may soon sound old-fashioned and dated. Slang and colloquialisms may be used in an article or story, but keep in mind that publication of such a piece must be shortly after its writing not to sound dated.

Concentrate on words that stand the test of time, words you use today and will use tomorrow.

We have suggested that the study of great authors, reading, in effect, is one of the best ways to add to your vocabulary. We have also suggested that a definite program through games, lists, and the reading of books on vocabulary development, will help. In this second suggestion might be included your constant awareness of a new word when you hear it spoken. Be on the alert when teachers, announcers, news commentators, lecturers and others use words unfamiliar to you. Make a note to look them up.

Write a 300-400 word composition on one of the following:

> "The Value of Words"
> "Three Ways to Increase Your Vocabulary"
> "Slang Has Its Place"

Many people learn to swim at an early age. I was in my early teens before I learned. Before my first lesson, I picked up a book on the art of swimming. I read it thoroughly, noted the various ways to hold arms and legs, and thought I had them mastered perfectly.

But I found out that no matter how much I'd read about swimming, I'd never become a swimmer until I got into the pool and practiced strokes. All the reading in the world meant nothing. I had to immerse myself in the unfamiliar element, the water, and start practicing under actual conditions.

Writing is no different. You can do all the reading you want, play all the word games you want, but you'll never become a writer until you get right down to it and write.

Keep practicing, keep writing, keep developing your technique.

The story is told of a young woman who came to a successful teacher of writing and asked for a formula for success. "Go home and write a million words," the teacher said, meaning that she should practice writing. She did and came back a few years later to give the teacher an autographed copy of her first book, explaining that it was the "last 100,000 of the million words."

So write, write some more, and keep writing. Write and utilize the words you have recently added. Try to work them into your new material. Note their effect. Do they help you get across the thought you really wanted?

Practice writing brief paragraphs. Rewrite them. Rewrite everything you do, trying to make the piece more effective, more dramatic, more meaningful. Become a connoisseur of words, an expert. Discern, for instance, the difference between "stubborn" and "opinionated." Look at your own work with great care, analyzing what you've said. Is it exactly what you meant?

Often a student is unhappy about comments I make on his paper. "But you got the wrong meaning!" is his cry.

Perhaps he had some other idea in his mind, but all I, as the reader of the paper, saw, was the printed word.

This matter of practice often discourages people. They hate to rewrite, and rewrite again. "It's boring," they say.

Yes, often it is. But consistent practice makes for expertness in any field.

Musicians practice hours on end. Athletes seem to perform brilliant feats without effort, but long hours of practice have preceded the playing of the game.

Larry Bearnarth, relief pitcher of the New York Mets, addressed one of our classes one day.

"In spring training down south, sometimes we spend two hours learning just how to field a bunt," he told us. "We just stand on the mound and time and time again the coach hits a bunt and we have to run off the hill, grab the ball and fire to first. It gets pretty monotonous after awhile, but it's part of the game."

Ball players may consider tiresome practicing the very same play hour after hour, but "it's all in the game." When the important moment occurs in a real contest, they have to move in quickly, scoop up the ball, and get the man out. To us in the stands, the play may look easy, but the maneuver may have taken hours upon hours of practice.

In order to make yourself continue putting words one after another, devise self-encouragement tricks.

Set goals for yourself. Make a game out of it. My son

takes several sheets of paper, tears them up into two-inch square pieces, then writes a number on them, from 1 to 25. He puts the highest number on top, the lowest on the bottom. Then he thumbtacks them to the wall.

As I write my stories and articles each summer, I pull off the numbers. Several weeks after I begin, I may be pulling off number 15. That means I see number 14 staring me in the face. I have fourteen more to go to reach my goal of 25. It may not work for you. It does for me.

Another way to encourage yourself is to prop up one of your published pieces, whether it's in the school paper, the local press, or somewhere else. Put this on your desk or in a place where it will challenge you to repeat your success.

When you become more adept, and checks start coming in, prop up the latest check as incentive.

These hints are simply methods used to keep going. Writing, remember, is a lonely game. No crowds or cheerleaders are rooting us on. No one has a gun at our heads urging us to race on. If you are a writer, however, you are creative. So work out tricks to keep yourself writing.

Some authors resolve not to eat an apple, drink a soda, or raid the refrigerator until they have written so many words. This is excellent self-discipline, and it usually works. It gets the words down, and that's what counts, the words in black and white, not simply in your head.

"Everyone is going to write the great American novel," someone once declared. "But few get up out of the easy chair and start." And starting is only part of it. It's the keeping on that counts.

Pick up the newspaper. Read a description of a sporting event, perhaps, mastering the facts. Then sit down, and from what you remember, rewrite the article. Or, better still, let the article simply be the start of some truly creative effort on your part.

You read about an injured ballplayer. The team had been depending upon his helping them win the pennant. Now he is out of the line-up.

Let your imagination go! Start a story or an article about a substitute who has to step in and take the big man's place. You weave in details of how the great Lou Gehrig got his chance years ago when Wally Pipp, the Yankee first baseman complained of a headache.

It didn't look like much of a substitution, a rookie going in temporarily to replace a veteran. It happens day after day in both the major and minor leagues. But Gehrig, Columbia University's contribution to the national pastime, was no ordinary rookie.

He refused to allow the veteran to step back into the line-up. Through his sensational fielding and hitting, Gehrig stayed in the position at the initial sack. In fact, he remained there for the incredible record of 2,130 consecutive major league contests.

But your imagination is soaring. You write about a different rookie, who goes in for the injured old-timer you've just read about. If you are writing a short story, maybe you tell about a discussion that the two players, the young and the old, have. You are practicing your writing skills, so don't worry how "corny" your plot might be.

You are not concerned with writing acceptable editorial material right now, though you do want to write it as well as you can. You are trying to unlimber your writing muscles, to get in the swing of putting words one after another, to express your thoughts. This item in the newspaper has simply been the spark to ignite your practice session. The main thing is to write, and that is just what you are doing.

If you don't feel eager to pluck something from the paper to get you going on a writing sprint, think about your experiences with your fellow students. Again, let your mind wander over incidents of the past months. Suppose a new student has come in.

Concentrate upon the thought of making adjustments in this world. Your mind might jump from that student, say, over to an experience you once had adjusting at a summer camp, or in a new home, or when you went traveling.

Maybe you were in the hospital. Remember how strange everything was? Then you went home, and again things at home even seemed strange for a while.

You might find yourself writing an article on "The Necessity of Adapting Yourself," "How to Get Along in Today's Changing World," or some other similar topic.

Maybe you are not very interested in your school newspaper's editorials. Why not sit down and practice writing one that you feel would interest more students? Perhaps you don't feel happy about some school situation—a lack of school spirit, or the need for a swimming pool, or boring assemblies.

How about writing 500 words or so on one such subject, expressing your innermost thoughts? It's good writing practice, and there is no substitute for getting right down into the water.

There are people all around you whom you see every day. Why not write a character sketch of a real or imaginary person? How about the perfect teacher? How about the perfect boy friend or girl friend?

Why not try your hand at "Five Things I'd Like to Find in a Friend"?

Often character sketches, though written only as practice, can be retained and reworked into material which is publishable.

One of my teachers gave an assignment to write an action-packed description of a boy walking through the woods with his German shepherd when a bear attacks. "Write what happens," the teacher suggested.

I did. Then I rewrote it and sold it to a youth publication. "Bob Davis' Decision" was the title of this earliest story of mine, the first of my fiction to be published.

So practice writing about men and women, boys and girls, friends, acquaintances, people in the news. But I cannot state too often the importance of starting to put down words consecutively, regularly.

Practice is the keynote in all that you do now. You want to become proficient in arranging your thoughts, in expressing yourself, in being able to write, not just when the spirit moves you, but whenever you command yourself to do it. Writers cannot wait for inspiration to strike; they must be able to put down words even when they are not in the right mood.

Not too long ago a tragedy occurred at a circus. Two members of a noted high wire act family were critically injured, and one died. But the family was still there the following week; the injured members had been replaced by others, and the act continued. "The show must go on." In the same way a writer must continue writing, under all conditions, at all times, whether or not he wants to.

How you go about enticing yourself to continue writing is up to you. Writers operate differently. But some sort of self-discipline must be involved. Some of us read the Scriptures, meditate, pray, and then write.

As you practice your writing, read what you have written. Reread it. You have to see just how master writers create their effect. How successful have you been, do you feel, in creating the effect you desired?

To evaluate one's own material is difficult. Still, a certain amount of objectivity can be achieved if one reads discriminately.

As you practice writing, analyze whether or not you are getting across the effect you want. Are you trying simply to give information? Do you try for interesting style?

Were you trying to make a character lifelike? In your character sketch did you make the person stand out, really seem human?

Whatever the objective you had in mind, do you feel you succeeded? If not, then rewrite. In rewriting, you often catch the almost elusive effect you are trying to achieve. And the rewriting is good practice. Replacing words with synonyms often alters a manuscript beyond recognition. Several words here and some more there, and you've now gotten across an idea much more dramatically.

One of the questions that may occur to you during this beginning period is whether or not you should share these practice exercises with anyone else. Since they are literally just that, practice sessions, keep them to yourself. If you decide to rewrite some, maybe an editorial for the school paper, or actually to use one for an optional composition, make sure you've gone over it thoroughly, with all the care possible, before showing the piece to someone else.

Also, remember that friends, even good ones, are poor critics. They will flatter you, tell you how good it is; and they may well be wrong, and often are.

A critic may be friendly, may know you well, but he is after all a critic. A teacher is that, too. He is interested in telling you what is wrong; he doesn't want simply to flatter you.

You want encouragement. All writers do. But you want the truth, given in as gracious a manner as possible, hopefully.

So keep practice sessions and their results to yourself, unless you think an "exercise" is good enough to see the light of day on a printed page. If you do, then write it again, adding a phrase here, brightening it up there, making sure that each line says what you want to say. Then submit it to editors.

Throughout this chapter, we have been talking about words, how to observe their effect in the works of great writers, how to practice achieving the effect you want in the mind of the reader.

Every writer is a custom-made job. A real writer cannot be an assembly line author. Automobiles, television sets, pieces of furniture, may be turned out by simply setting up the machines, but not good writing.

No two writers operate exactly the same, have identical backgrounds, the same goals, the same style. Critics have discussed and compared Hemingway's style and placed it alongside Stephen Crane's. They are very similar, but certainly they are still two distinct authors, very different from one another.

God has placed little ridges on the tips of your fingers. They make your fingerprints if you put ink on them and press them onto paper. Everyone's fingerprints are different. You are also unique as a writer, or will be when you sandpaper off the rough edges. Practice to build your vocabulary, and to use those words to become the very best writer you can be.

Write an optional composition (on any subject you wish) of 300-400 words or on one of the following:

"The Clock Never Stops"
"My Aspirations"

Write on the lines below any ideas for future writing which have occurred to you while reading this chapter:

Chapter 3

The Writer's Materials: Ideas

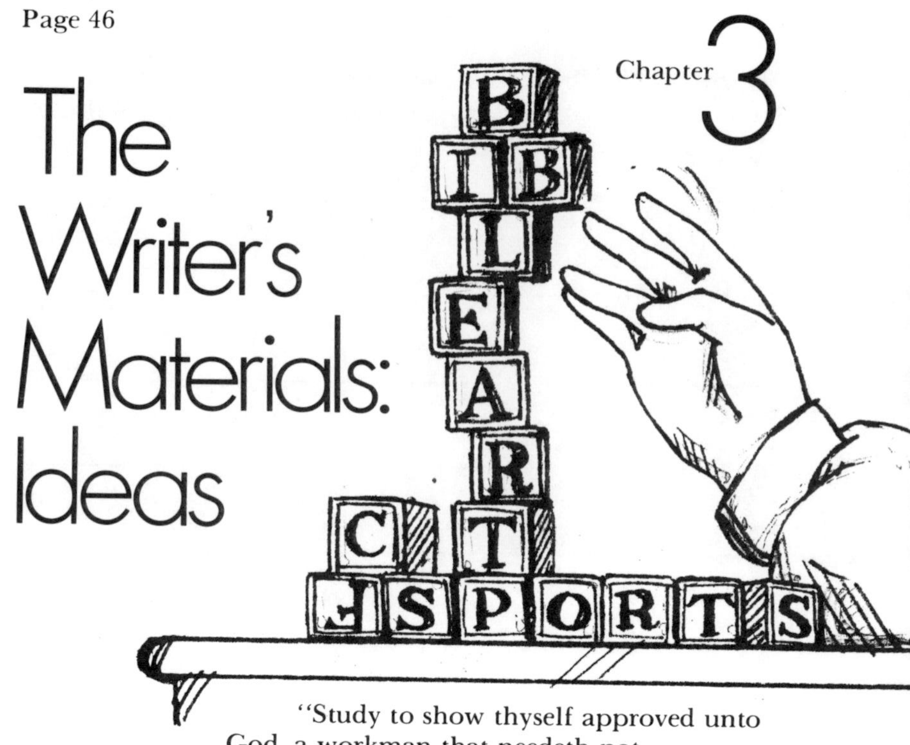

"Study to show thyself approved unto God, a workman that needeth not to be ashamed" *(II Timothy 2:15).*

You are a carpenter and you have a kit of tools. Is that enough to permit you to go to work? Not at all. You have to have something to work on, some lumber, wood to fashion into a bookcase, a table, a stool, a house.

As a writer you have your tools, words, and you can sit and examine and admire them all day long, but it won't get you anywhere, anymore than the carpenter who sits and admires his new saw or hammer or plane. Like him, you have not only to possess tools, you have to possess lumber on which to use them. In other words, as a writer you need the "lumber" of ideas.

This is a major problem for young or inexperienced writers. "Just what am I going to write about?" is a perennial cry.

In school, your composition titles or topics are usually given to you, to make you concentrate on one given idea. But editors don't go around strewing ideas about. In fact, editors are more hungry for ideas than you are.

To the question, what can I write about, the simple answer is "Anything at all."

From a perusal of popular magazines, we find that about anything that happened, happens, or might happen has been covered at some time or other. Old and new aspects of man's stay here on earth (or on the other planets!) seem to have been discussed in print. "There is nothing new under the sun" (Eccl. 1:9).

Yet some would-be writers try to catch these "idea-germs." They wonder just what method is followed by selling authors to come up with the essence of an article or a story.

Recently I took out carbon copies of some of my published stories and articles and analyzed their genesis, their birth. What I discovered is not world-shaking, but may be of some encouragement. Editor A.S. Burack, of *The Writer,* the oldest magazine for literary workers, founded in Boston in 1887, thought it was worth printing in his pages.

I discovered that an original idea came from one of three broad areas: Personal Experience, Observation, and Reading. Sometimes these seemed to merge or overlap, but basically, the stimulus from one of these areas started me placing paper in typewriter and hitting the keys.

Let's illustrate: At a church convention at Niagara Falls, the thought occurred to me: "Why not an article on them?" A trip to the Chamber of Commerce secured information, some "glossy pix" (pictures) and a very friendly welcome from local officials.

Niagara Falls is a trite subject. Hundreds of people had already written about the beauty of the cataract. If I expected ever to sell my article, it would have to have something new and different on the Falls. The new "slant," or approach, came from a visit I made to friends who had happened to see the Falls on TV. "It was the first time they ever focused cameras on the Falls live!"

This was the lead! A new twist to a hackneyed subject. TV and the Falls. It finally came out as "Cascade of Grandeur," and sold to *Upward,* a youth church magazine, with this opening:

> A network television sound-truck, wires wiggling from its interior like the antennae of a centipede, stood at one side of the road. Across the short, graveled path a TV cameraman pointed his walkie-talkie box at the roaring cataract. Suddenly, at the director's signal, a red light on the camera blinked on—and throughout America the majestic grandeur of mighty Niagara's Falls was flashed onto screens in a million living-rooms.

Friends from another city visited us and wanted to see Hyde Park, F.D.R.'s home. We drove the 90 miles to the shrine, and after seeing the unusual display of Roosevelt memorabilia, I wrote "Museum to My Friends," which *Boys Today* later published.

When my children were little, we used to make daily family devotions a sort of game with them. My folks, visiting from New York City, marveled at the way we easily enticed the youngsters away from their toys, and my sister suggested I write an article about the novel way we "played church" in our home. She felt that other families, wondering how to start religious instruction in the home, might appreciate it.

I wrote the article, and *Christian Herald* was enthusiastic about it. Years later when I met a professor at a theological seminary at a summer resort, he commented on the practicality of the article. He had read it a long time before but had not forgotten it.

I could duplicate a score of times how a personal experience led to the writing of an article. I took a one semester course in the History of Huntington on Long Island as an in-service course for teachers. When I completed it, I wrote "Nathan Hale's Heritage," for it was in nearby Halesite that the American patriot, a teacher-turned-spy, was captured by the British and later executed in New York City.

Time and time again, something I have experienced has led me to want to share the experience and has spurred me on to the typewriter, or to jot down notes.

What this writer has done, you, too, can do with a little effort and observation.

Which leads us to our second source, somewhat related to the first: Observation.

Driving down the highway out of Albany one day, I spotted a sign on the side of the road: "Fort Crailo, Home of 'Yankee Doodle.'" A few moments later we were at Fort Crailo, viewing the old well in the rear, where, it is said, the tantalizing song was written by an army surgeon during the French and Indian Wars. "The Story Behind

'Yankee Doodle,'" sold to *Young People*. If we had missed the sign on the road, we would probably have missed writing the article.

Once, walking down a street, I was attracted to a display of cultured pearls in a jewelry window. The result, after research, was "Gem of Mystery," which was given a two-page spread in *Vision,* another youth weekly. To illustrate the article, I secured black and white photographs from the Imperial Pearl Syndicate. In my article, I mentioned the Pearl of Great Price (Matt. 13:46).

"Eyes have they, but they see not" (Psalm 115:5). So the Scriptures speak of idols, false gods. But might they not apply to many of us, who "see but do not observe" as a famous detective of fiction, Sherlock Holmes, mentioned to his colleague?

Yet (lest one think this writer is Observation Personified), like one who had to leave London to appreciate Great Britain, I had to leave the Red Rose City of Lancaster, Pennsylvania, where Mennonites and Amish (the Pennsylvania Dutch) abound with their quaint ways and neat, checkerboard farms, before I could write an article about that region. "Red Roses and Pretzels" was the title of the published piece.

I was quicker to observe at Ocean Grove, New Jersey, one summer. There I noted an attractive little church where only children were allowed to worship. *Sunday Digest,* a large interdenominational weekly, ran "Chapel for Children."

Beyond personal experience and keen observation, perhaps one's reading, coupled with a "sense of the significant," as a college teacher of mine put it, is the best source of ideas.

You can look for the germ of an idea not only in books, magazines, and newspapers, but even in bills, those annoying communications which come around the first of the month.

For example, our telephone company encloses a little four-page folder each month. On the back page of this tract is always a brief, 75-word squib on some historical fact. When "Uncle Sam" was mentioned as originating in Troy, New York, I was off to the research corner of the Public Library. "Striped Hat and Whiskers," the story behind our country's "Uncle," emerged in the pages of another youth weekly.

In fact, the idea of writing a small article about the origin of this symbol of America led me to do further research. I finally came out with a series of six articles on "Emblems of America," including stories about not only Uncle Sam, but the Liberty Bell, the Statue of Liberty, the Stars and Stripes, the American Eagle, and the White House. *Woodmen of the World* purchased the series.

Even telephone bills can be blessings (Romans 8:28).

Just as Isaac Newton saw an apple fall, began to think about what made it fall, and came up with the theory of gravity, so the tidbits read in some paper, book, or periodical can launch one into the clouds of literary expression.

Somewhere I read a brief paragraph of an unusual restaurant in California where a series of rooms in the basement represent the Holy Land, and contain a life-size figure of the praying Christ, kneeling in Gethsemane. This is a great place for people to come for rest, relaxation, and inspiration in this disturbed world. "Garden of Influence" sold to *Sunday Digest,* and later, in a completely rewritten form, to a youth weekly.

I read a single, brief paragraph about a town that had created a statue to a bug! After correspondence, research, and some roughing out, I wrote "Monument to Misfortune," which described how this little creature almost wrecked the economy of a state, but in the final turn of events, brought greater prosperity.

A single paragraph in the *New York Times* led to "Accolade for Americans," about the unusual Youth Hall of Fame Michael Giacco was building for teenagers who made a name for themselves. *Futures,* Junior Chamber of Commerce monthly magazine, published it with photographs.

A short statement about a minister who had been called to the bedside of a dying girl who had taken poison, and after her death, had resolved to create a suicide-prevention agency, led to "Lifesavers on Land." It was the story of the "Save-a-Life League," a remarkable organization in New York City. This appeared in the young adult weekly, *Front Rank.*

Somewhere I ran across an item about a Texas newspaper, which, before the editorial rooms erupted in frenetic activity each morning, had a fifteen-minute devotional period led by different members of the staff. I secured more facts about this unusual daily and wrote "Five Star Faith."

A full-length article sprang from a single sentence in a newspaper about a man who collects postage stamps from all countries bearing religious scenes. "Scriptures on Stamps" sold to *Straight,* a boy-girl weekly published by the Standard Publishing Company in Cincinnati.

Need I say more? Reading can be the means of starting any intelligent person's brain working toward the creation of an entertaining, instructive, perhaps inspiring piece.

But beyond your personal experience, your observation, and your reading, someone might ask, aren't there ever other means for the development of ideas?

Yes, there are other ways to pick up ideas, or to stimulate thinking. I have simply described three basic ways ideas can come. Sometimes someone furnishes you with the idea.

Knowing I write, a friend once mentioned a layman out west, a local butcher so interested in building up the membership of his church that, like a minister, he visited every new family that came to town.

I wrote a letter to him, asking for information about his unusual pastoral visitations. He was very modest, and at first refused to tell me anything about himself, saying that he didn't feel it was worth publishing, or that it was even Christian to tell what he was doing, since some folks might think he was boasting.

I finally convinced him to give me the details of how he had led over 200 persons into closer fellowship with Christ and the Church. The result was an article, "Layman Extraordinary," which *Christian Herald* printed, with pictures of the unusual meat-merchant and evangelist.

A tip that a certain man owned five thousand different hymnbooks and pieces of sacred music resulted in a visit to him in upstate New York and the article, "Hymns Are God's Music."

But usually, because I am story-or-idea conscious, ideas come from my own grey matter. One must develop this facility.

Sometimes, you can just sit down, with a clean piece of copy paper shoved into your typewriter, and by forcing your mind, stumble upon something to write about. Anything is possible where that strange device, the human mind, is concerned.

Most writers, however, have thought about their subject before they have begun to write, and have a good idea of what they are going to put down on paper, whether it is pure fiction or fact.

As for myself, I have to have the title of my story or article or I'm lost. I have to know in what direction I'm going, what the story is to be about, even if it is fiction and I may not know the ending yet.

I've tried writing stories and articles without titles and they just don't jell. In this matter of titles, may I, while it

is "on the tip of my tongue," mention to you the process I follow in making up titles?

Let us assume that no title definitely appeals. Sometimes, strange to say, a ready-made title does come to mind, and I like it and use it. But often no definite name for the story or article arrives. I take a sheet of paper and write down about eight or ten titles, simply letting my mind have free rein.

Some time ago I wanted a title for a weekly column I was to write for the local newspaper. I was going to write about our professional ice hockey sextet which was to play at the arena. I put down a group of possible titles for the column: "At the Arena," "Hockey News," "Ice Items," "Hockey Highlights," and "Hockey Notes." We finally felt "Hockey Highlights" was the best, and that's what was used.

The same applies when I write fiction, or straight individual articles.

When you get ideas, wherever they come from, put them down in a folder, in a notebook, or on cards. Wherever and whenever they come, seize them!

Ideas are precious. "Nothing is so powerful as an idea which has emerged at the right time," someone has declared, and rightly.

That is why at the end of each of these ten chapters, we ask you to write down some new, original ideas. This creative writing handbook will be something of a writer's notebook if, when you have gone through the chapters, you will have put down ideas for future writing on these pages. You may well have some fifty new ideas to write about when you finish this book—fifty ideas that are yours and yours alone!

Write a 300-400 word composition on one of the following:

"The Strangest Moment I Ever Experienced" (Personal experience)

or "The Most Unusual (Person, Place, Event, or __________) I Ever Saw" (Observation)

or "A Newspaper Paragraph That Interested Me" (Reading)

In the first half of this chapter I detailed the sources of some of my original ideas. But by now you want to know how to develop your own ways of gaining new ideas.

Let me explain some of the methods we have been using in our classes to start the brain cells working on new thoughts, thoughts ultimately to result in a finished literary composition.

Usually the stimulus occurs through one of the five senses. Obvious? Yes. But the obvious is often paradoxically elusive.

Suffice to say that either through hearing, seeing, tasting, touching, or smelling the author gains an idea. In many instances the "eye-gate" opens the way to the stimulus that starts the thought waves.

In our classes, we tell students to use their eyes, to develop keen observation, and, while seeing, to make notes of ideas worth writing about.

For example, we go on a quiet walking tour of our school building. On this tour, I suggest that students observe what they see as they walk along, catching and mentally or literally recording something they've never noticed before.

It is remarkable how often students mention something they took for granted, or never even saw before. Their next writing assignment, then, is something they saw as they toured the building. And they come up with unusual papers.

In addition to observing the usual, they find themselves learning. For example, one of them began to appreciate the custodians of the school and grounds. "I never realized the amount of work that has to be done to give us a clean and usable school building," he said.

We visited the cafeteria, saw the preparations that go into feeding hundreds each day. Some of the class later wrote about their fascination with the huge, stainless steel pots, kettles, and other utensils used by the kitchen crew.

The girls had never been in the boys' shops and were intrigued by the automobiles the boys were working on, the lumber they were sawing and polishing, the electrical work. And of course, the boys were more than interested in our visit to the home economics rooms, especially since it was just before lunch hour.

The tour is only one method used to stimulate students' thinking in our creative writing class. Regardless of the size of a school, the method can be utilized. If your class cannot go on a full-period tour, you can go alone. Resolve to look at your school with the eyes of a newcomer, a stranger who sees it for the first time.

If you resolve to do so, you can see your own home, church friends, yourself, in such an analytical way. And what you will see may amaze you. You may have just been dimly aware before, now you truly observe.

Another "sight" or "seeing" exercise that gives students a chance to develop their observation of the world all around them, is to ask them to write about something they see outside the classroom window.

I will never forget the almost poetic quality of a composition written about a tree outside our window. The student used the tree as a symbol of the four seasons of man's life: spring, summer, autumn, and winter (Ecclesiastes 3:1).

She wrote of the budding of the tree in early spring, then made references to the younger years of man's life. She proceeded to describe nature's summertime, man's "summertime," autumn and winter.

Her inspiration had been a thoughtful look out of a classroom window. You can do the same. It may be the sky you see, or the ground, or grass or concrete. Whatever it is, use your imagination on it.

I also ask students to write a composition sparked by some object they see within the room (excluding the teacher!). I have received stimulating pieces on the flag, the clock with its lesson of time passing (one student wrote "where will I be five years from now?"), the blackboard, and even the wastebasket. All these objects have been the starting point of an interesting composition. Training the imagination is a lifelong discipline.

Note that some material object, some stimulus from the outside world was the starting point for activating the imagination. This is the secret to putting one's mind to work: placing something before it by means of the senses to galvanize the brain.

We also ask our students simply to stare at their hands for a few minutes. Then we conduct a brief class discussion: tell us of one thing a hand or a pair of hands can do. We list these on the blackboard:

Play a piano
Operate on a human being
Build a bookcase
Write a poem
Wave to a friend
Pitch a baseball
Brush the teeth
Hold a small baby
Point out an unusual sight

After the suggestions are on the blackboard, we ask the

students to select one action and write a composition about it. Try it yourself, if you want a stimulus to write (Ecclesiastes 9:10).

For sight-stimulus, we may present a photograph, or a picture from a magazine or newspaper. We usually have several piles of these around the room. Students are asked to leaf through the pictures, then write about anything appealing to them. All that the picture is supposed to do is to create some image in the writer's mind, something that will cause him or her to focus upon an idea and begin writing.

Like some of the preparations on the market to start charcoal going at a picnic, the photos do just that, get the writing started. Students are not merely to describe the picture, but to utilize it to write something constructive.

One of the photos used has been that of an Indian, a chief standing alone, gazing into the distance. One of the students who saw it was moved to write a very challenging piece about the way the Indian has been treated ever since the white man landed on these shores.

A picture of a locomotive led a student to write a lengthy piece about transportation today.

To use another one of the five senses, I have read from articles and then have asked students to continue the story or article. Consider the following:

> "Be careful with that light!" Dr. Carver Cranston's voice sounded strangely hollow.
>
> Dick Henry, preceding the noted archaeologist, nodded. "Don't worry! I've waited too long for this trip to mess it up now!"
>
> The long, narrow passageway wound dizzily before the youth. Shadows bounced eerily around on walls and ground as the light advanced through the cavern. From his reading, Dick was well aware that the first moments of exploring a cave were always the most dangerous. Birds, bats, reptiles, and other inhabitants

could make an explorer's life extremely hazardous.
Suddenly - - - - - -."

You pick up the story from there. This is the start of "Cavern of Danger," a short story I wrote, which appeared in the youth weekly *Upward.*

When you continue the yarn, I know it won't be the same as the one I wrote, for no two authors write exactly alike. But it will be good practice for you.

So, if you don't know what to write about, start reading a story, drop it, and write your own ending. Don't let that other author grip you too tightly with his story—you don't want to read straight on to the end! You're not reading for entertainment. You want the story's beginning to stimulate your writing. That's why it is usually best to have the teacher or someone else start reading. He or she will stop after a few paragraphs and leave you to your writing.

Some of these methods may seem odd, but all of them are being used with success. Their goal is one: to get students to write.

Another sense very amenable to motivating writing is the sense of sound. For a portion of a period we play records, "mood music" or background music, trying not to use any familiar songs too easily identifiable. The idea is to let the imagination of the class have full rein as the sounds of the orchestra are wafted into the room. Then, no matter what the music may have been written for, ballet, movie, or chamber music, say, the student conjures up images, then writes.

Music may stimulate one student to think of a quiet scene on a lake, another a walk through the woods, another a personal experience completely unrelated to the music.

At any rate, the music, entering through the "ear-gate," captures the imagination and the words start.

Some of our students have found another method of

great value. I bring in a box of cookies and give each student a single piece to munch on. As he munches, he is asked to make any notes he wishes. After he finishes the cookie, he writes his composition. The gastric juices, beginning to flow, help the flow of words.

Primarily, what we have been describing are devices to initiate thinking which leads to writing. Yet there are far more subtle reasons for using these techniques.

For as the student does make use of his senses, he is exercising them, and that is just what the writer must do. He must become keenly familiar with and alert to all the world around him. His sense of sight must be so trained that he sees what the unobservant miss, things that add color and individuality to writing.

"Oh, I never thought of that!" someone might declare as he reads an unusual magazine article. But the writer did think of it, and probably was stimulated to do so by keen observation.

When I heard the fire siren go off one night, I began to think of the volunteer firemen who jump out of their beds to answer alarms. I did some research and wrote an article about the "vamps," as they are called.

In a large department store, I heard an announcement over the public address system. I later interviewed the man who is called "the broadcaster" in that store, and wrote an article about him and his unusual vocation.

People with a pronounced sense of taste often secure jobs tasting or writing about foods. And there is also a place for the writers who know how to describe exotic or unusual dishes for readers always in search of new recipes.

Walk down the halls of your school and try out your olfactory sense. You may smell new wood as you pass the boys' shops, or gasoline as they work on a car, or paint.

Or try the science wing. (Be prepared for anything here.)

Such jaunts through your own school or neighborhood will do much to develop the senses. You will find yourself more alert to what is happening around you, more alert to the possibilities for stories and articles.

Becoming conscious of the world around you, however, is not enough. While it is true that you can write about anything under the sun, you also must cultivate your imagination, your thinking, to come up with new angles.

Some people are born with vivid imaginations and are sensitive to the possibilities around them. Others are not so fortunate. They must keep exercising to keep imagination flexible and in use.

The writer who entertains, challenges, stimulates, inspires, is one who combines stimuli and imagination to produce his finished product. Whether he has to keep prodding his imagination, or is a lucky creature who by nature has an active one, no matter.

Editors will not be concerned whether or not your imagination is one you have had to keep needling. They will look only at the work on the page.

When he was a youth, James A. Garfield, the martyred President, went to Williams College. He was so poor he worked his way through, farming, preaching, doing anything he could to complete his college career.

His widowed mother in Ohio once sent him a note with some shirts she had mended at the elbows. She was sorry that the shirts were so repaired, that the family was so poor it couldn't provide young James with new or at least unmended shirts.

Garfield wrote back, "Don't worry about the mended shirts, Mother. When I complete my college work no one will say 'There's Jim Garfield. He always wore mended shirts.' They'll say 'There goes Jim Garfield. He has a college degree.' "

No, editors don't care how you prod your imagination. They don't care whether or not you walked back and forth ten times before you wrote one word, or the phrases tumbled forth like a mighty waterfall. Get it down! That's what counts!

Just as the words we talked about in the previous chapter are essential, so the writer's ideas are essential. The words are tools. The ideas are the materials the tools work on. Together they result in a *Paradise Lost* or a *Tale of Two Cities.* Add your contribution to the world's great literature by combining your senses, your mind, and your imagination!

Write a 300-400 word composition on one of the following:

"A Section of My School I Didn't Know About"
"A View from the Window"
An optional topic based on something you Saw, Heard, Smelled, Tasted, or Touched

---

Write on the lines below any ideas for future writing which have occurred to you while reading this chapter:

Chapter 4

The Paragraph

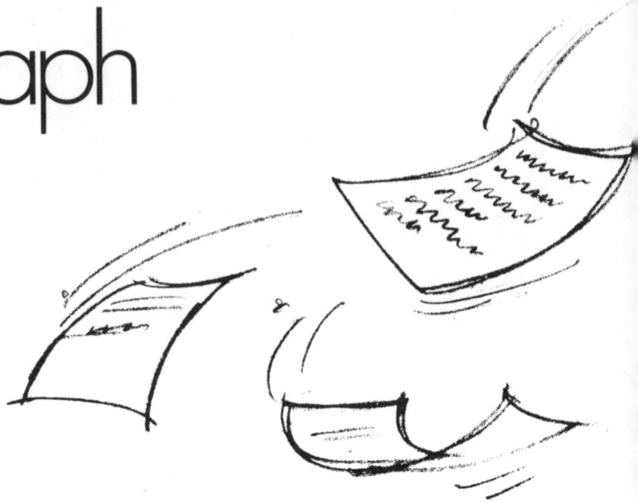

"Thy word is a lamp unto my feet,
and a light unto my path" *(Psalm 119:105).*

One of the most stimulating, inspiring men I have ever met appeared one summer at a writer's conference at Chautauqua, New York. He was Edward Weeks, editor of *Atlantic Monthly.*

Mr. Weeks first spoke to the assembled writers and would-be authors, offering advice from his background as a writer and editor. "Increase your facility to write!" he urged. "Write constantly, regularly."

He told how Sinclair Lewis, one of our country's great novelists, held a regular job, as many writers do before they turn fulltime authors. After the long day's work, Lewis would come home and write for several hours each night, regularly, night after night.

This was the point Mr. Weeks hammered away on. Lewis practiced his writing regularly, night after night. "Don't allow writing lapses," Mr. Weeks suggested. "Keep going. Don't wait until you are in the mood."

When we come, then, to these practice sessions for you as a writer, keep this in mind. The great writers kept at it, everlastingly, finally to produce publishable copy.

Time is usually a big factor with students. You have many activities. That is where the practice in writing brief paragraphs may be just the ticket. You can just fit it into what a great teacher-preacher-missionary, Dr. Frank Laubach, calls "the chinks of time," those few moments that fall your way when you have nothing else pressing.

Into these small intervals the paragraph can fit nicely. You are not trying to write a 10,000 word short story, or even a 1,000 word one. You are just using these few moments to develop facility.

Years ago I studied shorthand. The instructor urged us to make use even of moments when we didn't have a pen, pencil or paper. "On a bus, in a car, waiting for a class to start, on any occasion," he urged, "place one hand in the palm of the other and practice your shorthand strokes."

"Writing shorthand" in any place, at any time, the brief, disjointed words or phrases of previous lessons would become so familiar we would have them at our fingertips, literally, when it came to writing them down in a court or office.

In other words, fill in those little "chinks of time."

If you don't have an hour to write, use ten minutes. Grab a piece of paper and start writing a paragraph. It's good practice for any writer.

Of course, some say this is only part of the game. Paragraphs are too brief to be considered finished products. To such thinking, I'd respond that many times a paragraph well written is the start of a longer piece, which could turn into a story or article fit for publication.

Just as part-time or leisure time activities or avocations may turn into full time jobs, so little paragraphs written during one's free moments can be kept and developed into full length products. After all, paragraphs are the foundation for all writing.

Discussions of paragraphs and their length often lead to differences of opinion. "How high is up?" the comedian asked. "How long should a paragraph be?" is a question just as debatable.

Read Charles Dickens and you'll find some paragraphs as long as a page. Read most modern authors, and a paragraph is sometimes a single sentence.

Under certain conditions, the single sentence paragraph

may be perfectly in order. Certainly it is in writing dialogue. Every time a different person speaks, the author must start a new paragraph.

You might even have a single word as a paragraph. And each time another person, another character expresses himself, even if he does it with a "Huh?" or "Eh?" or "What?" you will have to start indenting again.

Usually a paragraph is a group of sentences developing one small topic. The "topic sentence" more or less announces, or succinctly states, the topic of the paragraph. Since it usually appears at the start of the paragraph, it is somewhat like the "lead" of a newspaper story, written "block-paragraph style." The lead can be run and the rest of the story eliminated if the paper doesn't have the space, and the main facts still will be there.

When you have stated your topic sentence, build upon it. Offer examples, illustrations to back up opening statements. Compare or contrast, thus solidifying the opening.

Suppose you have written the opening, topic sentence: "Baseball has been called America's national pastime." How would you continue?

You might use the chronological development, showing how the game has evolved over the years since Captain Abner Doubleday is believed to have started it in Cooperstown, New York, back in 1839. You might point out that the game was played by amateurs until the famous Cincinnati Red Stockings, the first professional ball team, was organized. You might then trace the origin of other professional teams, bringing the history of the sport up to date, also showing in what other ways our national game has developed.

On the other hand, you might want to argue against this opening, topic sentence, explaining why you think the sport is not worthy of being the national game. You might prefer to point out that other games are creeping up on it, particularly basketball, now supposedly played by far more schools than any other game. Or you might want to indicate other reasons why you refute this statement that the game ranks as a "national pastime."

If you don't employ a chronological arrangement in your paragraph, or the argumentative, using contrast or comparison, you might want to list certain facts about the game to show why it is called the national pastime. In this third way you will build your case for the topic sentence, perhaps, by pointing out that (1) more people watch this sport either live or on television than any other; (2) it is truly an American sport, whereas football and ice hockey, for example, were not originated in the States; and (3) no other sport has such a far-flung system of minor and major leagues.

In effect, then, we can build up a factual, formal, expository paragraph in three ways: chronologically, argumentatively (comparison and contrast) or the listing of supporting facts. We say formal and expository paragraphs because there are other kinds you can write, such as descriptive pieces, which are somewhat related to the expository, and dialogue.

Your practice in writing paragraphs will be of great value to you in writing longer pieces. One teacher I know remarked that if you have mastered the art of writing good paragraphs, you have mastered much of the technique of writing. This is true only to a point. One might be able to write brilliant expository paragraphs and still not be able to give a piece of fiction the "twist" that makes it worth publishing.

There is a big difference between knowing how to fry eggs and bacon and how to prepare a whole dinner. The difference is that between the "short-order" cook in a diner and the chef of a metropolitan hotel. The chef usually makes four or five times as much as the short order cook. The diner cook has only limited knowledge of cooking, the chef a vast fund.

Just as the diner cook finds his knowledge might be the stepping stone to grander places, so the fundamental knowledge you as a budding author acquire with your paragraphs will stand you in good stead. Practice is the name of the game. If you can't play a whole ball game, isn't it worthwhile at least to play a few innings?

Avoid the double danger of Scylla and Charybdis, the rocks and the whirlpool, when writing paragraphs. You don't want to write so lengthy and boring a paragraph that your reader is bogged down. On the other hand, you don't want to write too thin a one that is not convincing. A two sentence paragraph, with five or six words in each sentence, might be too short and ineffective. A 300 word paragraph with solid facts being marshalled all along the way might prove equally ineffective. Try for the middle road.

Many expository paragraphs have the same characteristics as longer compositions, in that they usually have a beginning, a built-up middle or body, called the development, and a solid conclusion. The starter in this type of paragraph is the topic sentence. The body is the accumulated facts, incidents, or arguments you write to back up the opening or to refute it. The final statement is the summary, the "tag-line," as some writers call it, or "clinching sentence."

The final sentence, in far too many paragraphs written by students, is often weak. Typical is the kind which may simply say: "And these are my reasons for not wanting to go to school six days a week." These are usually wasted words. A clincher sentence for such a topic might better read: "And I am not the only student who feels this way about going to school six days a week."

The latter of the two concluding statements would lend itself to a good transitional statement for another paragraph if this were to be developed into a full-fledged composition. Transitional sentences are important for they continue an author's thought only sketchily presented in one paragraph, into the next.

When you are writing individual paragraphs, for practice, keep in mind the possibilities for development into longer pieces.

It has often been stated that one of the best professions for creative writers, as a preliminary to short stories, long articles, and novels, is journalism. We have mentioned the "lead" which is written for most news articles. All of the important information the reader wants to know about an event is contained in that original, introductory paragraph.

> A two-yard plunge with eight seconds remaining earned the Millford High eleven a 28-24 come-from-behind win yesterday afternoon over Norris High before 3,500 screaming fans.

In the following paragraphs the sportswriter fills in the details. As he writes, he is simply developing the original (in this case a full newspaper paragraph) "topic sentence."

The tight writing of newspaper leads is excellent practice for beginning writers. Think about some sport you are interested in. Practice writing imaginative leads for a game. Or, if you know of a game recently played, practice writing your lead. As a real newspaperman might, try to squeeze all the "Who-What-When-How-or-Why" as well as "Where" into the opening.

Often such leads are not what the truly creative writer would call a complete paragraph. Journalistic writing is somewhat different from that of the novel or short story. It is very closely allied with the writing of articles, though, and on some newspapers the "feature article" is just a step away from a straight magazine article.

One of the dangers in practicing the writing of paragraphs is that the student may become so enamoured of merely placing words down in order to say he has written a paragraph, that he may not create a unified thought. Lacking unity, a paragraph tends to be confusing, ineffective, boring. The reader's mind wanders, the thread is difficult to recapture, and the author fails to retain the eye and mind of the reader.

For unity, write only statements relevant to your topic sentence. This is the best way to avoid going off on a dreary side road.

No writer wants his readers to wonder how on earth a particular remark came to be placed where it is, to say, "I thought we were discussing the merits of these two automobiles; why did we suddenly start talking about price?" The price might come later, in another sentence or paragraph, but at the moment, only the ability of the cars to perform, not the costs, is relevant.

So write relevantly. Keep your thoughts on the one main idea expressed by the topic sentence, and stick with it.

All of what we say is to be applied only to the serious, formal, expository paragraph. If you are writing dialogue, as we stated before, or a humorous piece, even satire, different rules apply. In fact, breaking most of the rules usually is the modus operandi of a humorous writer.

We are thinking of authors such as Robert Benchley, who once in describing an opera, mentioned in the middle of his paragraph another character who comes in, has nothing whatever to do with the plot, looks around, and walks off the stage again. Such irrelevant characters, or

facts, might be used for comic effect, but not if you are writing serious material.

Speaking of humor, let us suggest that if you are thinking of writing it, whether in a weekly composition, or for publication, be careful! Humorous writing is not the easiest. It often boomerangs on the author who may think his "cute" remarks are really risible, when they may simply fall flat or misfire.

The written word is not the easiest way to make people laugh. Only truly comic and experienced authors can. Everyone can't be a Benchley, or a Goodman Ace. At one time the latter was said to be paid $8,000 a week to write the humorous dialogue or copy for the Perry Como television program. No one pays this amount of money for easily written material that may not be sure-fire.

This teacher would be the last to tell you never to attempt humor. I only admonish that if you think by simply breaking all the rules of professional writing, you will be writing funny stuff, don't do it!

Stick to writing interesting and, if not serious material, at least that which is logical and follows the rules. Your chances of making the grade will be much better than if you try to defy tradition. Later attempt the iconoclastic road if you will.

Since one is not always the best judge of his efforts, make sure that occasionally the better of these practice paragraphs are read to the class. A regular part of the Creative Writing class program might be to have a certain day set aside for the analysis of such brief pieces.

During such "moments of truth" you may find your "humorous" remarks were really not that funny. Your classmates' statements often come as a distinct jolt.

"I didn't 'get' that point about the horse and buggy."

"What did he mean by the Achilles heel?"

"Was that paragraph supposed to be funny?"

Whether you try to write funny material or not, have

your classmates evaluate what you have written. To hear the consensus of the class is very instructive.

And don't let sometimes disparaging remarks knock you. down "for keeps." It's all practice, like a scrimmage before the real game. It's only to sharpen you up for the real work ahead. The real work for you might be a novel, a play, or a magazine piece. So write the paragraph—for criticism by your class or teacher—and "take it all with a grain of salt."

Write a topic sentence, followed by a good developing series of sentences (a full expository paragraph) about any three of the following:

"My Favorite Sport"
"Our Nation's Greatest Problem"
"What I Like about School"
"Life on Mars"
"Flying Is for the Birds"
"The Value of a College Education"
"Listening to Parents"
"Extracurricular Activities"

So far we have discussed words, ideas, and paragraphs. But words form sentences, and sentences become paragraphs. Your ideas are expressed primarily in sentences.

Although this is not a grammar handbook, some time must be spent discussing this group of words called a sentence. From your study of grammar you will remember that technically a sentence is a group of words expressing a complete thought. Briefly, as far as their ideas or purposes are concerned, sentences are of four kinds:

1. the declarative
2. the imperative
3. the interrogative
4. the exclamatory

The creative writer will be thoroughly familiar with all kinds. Just as he will introduce variety into his writing by the use of compound and complex sentences, he will make use of all kinds of sentences from the declarative to the exclamatory. He will, however, use these only when they fit.

The writer who strews exclamation points throughout his narrative to try to give the effect of much dramatic action, will be labeled amateur. The use of exclamatory points and exclamatory sentences must be sparing. The effective writer will not need to "telegraph" to the reader the fact that what has been said was exciting. The context will indicate that.

Nevertheless, since sentences are the foundation stones of paragraphs, and we are talking about writing paragraphs, for practice and for possible use later as parts of completed pieces, let us consider each of these four kinds.

The declarative sentence is the one used in the majority of cases, the one we should study the most. It occupies most of the space in all forms of writing: reports, essays, novels, short stories, or newspaper articles. Strangely enough, many experts in the field claim this is the area in which students often are weakest. You need have no such weakness. In fact, in writing practice paragraphs, you can have fun revising your declarative sentences.

The declarative sentence is a group of words that expresses a fact. "My high school has just opened its new building." It is concluded with a period, unlike the exclamatory or interrogative sentence.

The declarative sentence makes a statement. And when you write, you can make any statement you wish. You can enjoy yourself in having your last place team win the pennant, "shellack" the league leaders, or take the World Series. The truth may be otherwise, but you are simply playing with sentences.

The joy of creative writing is that the words are yours. You can manipulate them any way you wish. You can put the accent on any part of the facts you wish.

You may have often joked about a simple statement, repeating it each time, accenting a different word each time for a different effect. "*John* threw the ball." "John *threw* the ball." "John threw the *ball.*"

In the same way you can manipulate a sentence, place the accent in different places, give a different effect. Play around with a statement about a character moving into a situation in different ways. "Slowly, carefully, cautiously, quietly, he stole across the living room floor, pausing from moment to moment to listen for sounds from upstairs." That's one effect, the accent on quiet maneuvering.

Can you rewrite it several ways? Sure you can. Here's one: "He wiped his moist brow as he listened, wondering whether there was anyone upstairs, then started to walk quickly, jerkily across the living room floor." Can you improve on that? Of course you can, according to what kind of effect you want to create for your paragraph, your story.

Here is where knowledge of grammatical principles comes in. Your knowledge of such things as infinitive and prepositional phrases, adverbial and adjectival clauses, and other aspects of the technical, structural side of our language can be put to use to give the effect wanted.

"Down we went into the dark cave, past the last marker, through the winding passage, to the edge of the precipice." Note the series of prepositional phrases in this sentence. How would you reword the sentence, using say, adverbial clauses? It is good practice to try other versions for other effects.

A word of caution, however. In your effort to write effective sentences, try not to become so interested in fancy phrases and dramatic language that you begin to write

"purple paragraphs," flowery passages so obviously artificial, insincere, and roundabout that they annoy the reader. Don't try to imitate a Shakespeare. Sound like a good, modern American writer, expressing himself in the acceptable, standard language of the day in which he lives. Avoid what has been called "overwriting." Say what you want to say simply, so that it is immediately understood.

Euphemisms are part of flowery language. Today we call the undertaker a "mortician," or as one book suggests, "a grief therapist." The former janitor or custodian is now "a disposal engineer"! Before long, baseball players may be called "spherical scientists"!

Yet you do want to avoid dull, plodding, pedantic

phraseology. You want to keep the reader moving along, interested. You want to find new phrases to express old ideas. For most of the ideas we write about are old. When we come to the short story section of the book we'll talk about the "Thirty-Six Plot Situations" that supposedly form the basis of all fiction ever written.

In order to avoid "stale" writing, stay away from clichés, phrases once fresh and original, but through repeated usage, now boring and antiquated, such as "the briny deep," "a bolt from the blue," "cheeks as red as apples."

If you really want to make a list of these "bromides," view some of the westerns on TV. You'll be able to fill a page or two just from seeing one show.

"This town isn't big enough for both of us." "Yeah, what are you going to do about it?"

Create fresh, new metaphors, similes or hyperboles, the figures of speech that brighten up writing. Become adept at expressing yourself in figurative language. Develop a distinctive style in this manner that will set you apart from less imaginative writers.

Here's an illustration of simile from "Deep Water Danger," a scuba story I wrote for *Straight,* a youth weekly.

> The old ceremonial urn was covered with greenish-black mud as he lifted it for inspection by the light of his lamp. Seaweed dangled from it, like an ivy plant that might hang in a kitchen or a window of a home. He had found the object of their summer's search.

Dreaming up your own figures of speech, metaphors, similes, and hyperboles can be part of the fun of creative writing. You may have read of the expression "as big as a house" (hyperbole). Try to say it yourself in an equally dramatic but original way.

Speaking of expressing yourself in a dramatic manner, avoid what has been called "gobbledygook." This is the confusing, unclear statement that has to be read several times to be understood. Don't say: "Since the evidence of our senses indicates that a conflagration is raging, it is necessary for us to vacate the premises as soon as possible." Just yell "Fire! Everyone out!"

Boil down your sentences. Eliminate the dead wood that discourages the reader. Why say, "Because of the fact that" when "because" alone does the trick?

When you write your declarative sentences, experiment. Use figurative language, but don't overwrite. Write clearly, effectively, interestingly—and succinctly.

In addition to declarative sentences, you will want to be able to handle the interrogative. A question neatly inserted into any kind of writing often breaks up the solidity of the prose enough to make the reader want to go on. Even in straight, expository writing, the use of a rhetorical question is of immense value. By rhetorical question, I mean one that doesn't require the answer to be thought about for it is plainly implied in the question.

For instance, "Since these facts are so appalling, will we give up the game? No, Americans always play it out to the end, leaving it to the final decision of the umpire."

Interrogatory sentences, always concluding with a question mark, ask a question, whether or not, as in the case of the rhetorical question, an answer is forthcoming.

Usually, of course, a question demands an answer, and the reader expects to find the author submitting it in the following lines.

"Who had the nerve to use my pen?" Howie glanced at each of his three friends in turn.

"I'm sorry, Howie, I did," Ralph finally admitted.

As in the case of the declarative sentence, you can have enjoyment practicing writing questions, too. Often, beginning a story or a paragraph with a question, a "tickler," gains the attention of the reader.

In short stories such an opening sentence is known as the "narrative hook"; it "reaches out and grabs the reader," arrests his attention. Momentarily he is caught by the possibility of an answer.

As in fiction, a question might start an essay, too, or even a speech. Think of the reaction of your audience if you were to stand in front of them after being introduced, and ask, "Want to make a million dollars quickly and easily?" You can be sure you'd have their interest.

Practice writing questions. In fact, keep in mind the device of starting with a question. Don't overdo it; don't start everything you write with a query. Use this method only occasionally.

The imperative sentence is nothing more than a command. You will find use for this, in many cases, in short stories. "Put down that stick! Stand over there!" You can imagine a dozen similar examples.

This form of sentence, too, must be used sparingly. What kind of story could you create if every other sentence were a command? (Now, don't look for an answer to that—it's a rhetorical question!)

A milder form of command, in effect, a request, usually forms an imperative sentence. "Please enclose fifty cents in stamps when sending your order." "Call me when you get the time."

Although we have used exclamation points above ("Put down that stick! Stand over there!"), these commands, according to the way spoken, could be ended with periods.

When it comes to expressions or exclamations indicative of strong feeling, usually the exclamation point is used. Exclamatory sentences almost always end with such a mark. Again, this kind of statement can get you into danger if overused.

A discussion of interrogative, imperative, exclamatory and declarative sentences leads us to the different kinds of sentence structures. Simple, complex, and compound sentences lend variety to one's writing and keep the reader reading.

Now that they are progressing in their education, some students may feel that simple sentences should be shunned. They were all right for beginners but such "childish statements" should be avoided. Nothing could be farther from the truth. The short, pithy, simple sentence has its place as much as does the longer, complex or compound sentence.

Variety, not monotony, is what you seek in your literary endeavors. Use all forms of sentences to tell your story. Don't snobbishly turn your back on briefer statements. Often a series of terse, factual, simple sentences is very effective, such as in fast moving, dramatic action:

"He jumped to his feet. Dalton stood in the doorway. He was smiling insolently. 'Didn't expect to see me today, did you?' "

The almost jerky, simple sentences give a motion picture effect of quickly flashed scenes, one after another.

So, use the simple sentence when it will be effective. Together with the compound and complex, the simple sentence gives you all the ammunition you need to stock your "paragraph arsenal."

In your writing of practice paragraphs, and in fashioning sentences to fill such paragraphs, do just that, write sentences. Yes, you will often find professional writers, experienced men and women, using fragments, but you should avoid the use, except in dialogue. Leave the use of the fragment to more experienced writers. You are still "learning the trade," so stick to standard procedure. Write complete sentences.

To sum up: develop your writing skills by writing paragraphs in those slots of time whenever you find them. Write about anything and everything that interests you—sports, hobbies, school, personal relations, science, reading, history, anything. Write about some things that don't interest you, see whether or not you can expand your mind. Force yourself to write.

Develop good topic sentences. Fill in the general suggestion of the topic sentence with lucid, logical statements, illustrations. Don't give up writing practice paragraphs. Some day one of them may grow into a full-length piece that will be published in a newspaper, magazine, or book.

Write a paragraph of about 150 words on any three of the topics below or any other three topics in which you are interested. Create an interesting topic sentence. Make sure you include, for variety's sake, at least one simple, one compound, and one complex sentence in each paragraph.

"The Season I Like Most"
"Science Today"
"Man's Greatest Triumph"
"My Family's Most Interesting Trip"
"Part-time Jobs"
"Animals I Have Known"
"The Year 2000"
"Boy Meets Girl"

Have any new ideas occurred to you while reading this chapter? Write them below for further consideration later:

____

____

____

____

____

____

____

____

Chapter 5

The Short Story

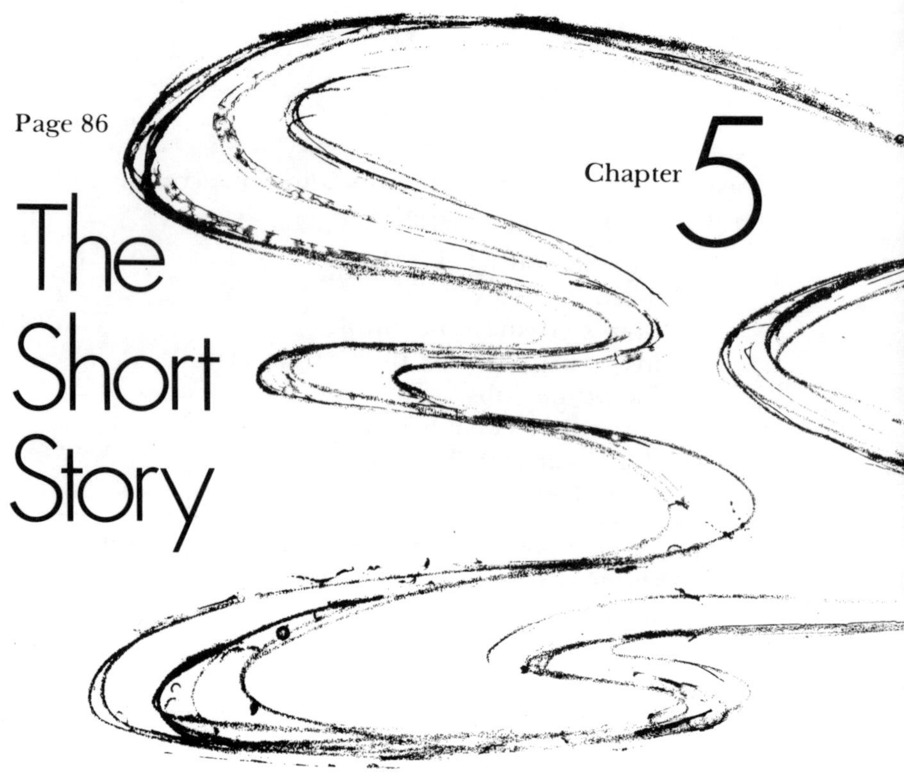

"And he spoke this parable
unto them, saying. . ." *(Luke 15:3).*

Most beginning writers are intrigued with fiction. And well they might be. For the new author a short tale has many advantages. He can fashion any kind of character he wishes, place him in any setting he desires, mold any kind of plot.

When you write fiction, the imagination has no limit. You can set your story on distant Mars, down in the depths of the ocean, or here on earth. Your story can take place in a high school gym or out on a baseball field or hockey rink.

Your hero (or heroine) can be tall, short, thin, fat, or average. The girl in the story can have hazel eyes, a baby's

complexion, or a freckled face with brown eyes. She can be wealthy and snobbish or poor and humble. Character is up to you.

When he sits down to write a story, a vicarious thrill awaits every amateur writer. He may never have been a great swimmer, but in his story he can win the Olympic free-style race and break the world's record! She may never have amounted to much as a tennis player, but she's a champ in the story she writes.

The writer of fiction is like Aladdin with his magic lamp. All wishes can become fact. You want to be the best dancer in school, the best athlete, the best actor in the dramatics group? Be your own guest, simply make your hero or heroine just that! In effect, you are living out that desired role in the characters you create out of your imagination.

There are 26 letters in the English language. It has long amazed some people how writers take those "squiggles" and manipulate them to evolve believable characters.

For instance, Sherlock Holmes. Remember that when A. Conan Doyle fashioned this fictitious master-detective, Holmes was nothing but an idea in his creator's mind. He did not exist until A. Conan Doyle put him on paper. Yet today many actually think Holmes was a real person.

This is the art of the storyteller, to so describe a character, place him in such realistic situations, have him react so naturally, that the reader believes in his reality.

Doyle is not alone in his development of characters considered real persons. Earle Stanley Gardner, who created "Perry Mason," also constructed a "person" accepted as real. Mason is only a figment of Gardner's mind. He never existed until the author gave him life on his pages.

Some years ago I decided to write a story with a teenage boy as hero. He was, I decided, to be interested in archaeology.

What should I call him? I remembered my cousin in Connecticut. His name was Henry, a name he had never liked, so we had started to call him "Dick." I put the two names together, and "Dick Henry" is the name I used.

Dick appeared in "Cavern of Danger," later in "Mountain Peril," still another time in "Deep Water Danger." His older colleague is Dr. Carver Cranston, a professor of archaeology, who invites Dick to join him on some of his expeditions. Both Dr. Cranston and Dick Henry don't really exist—except in my mind (and in my readers', I hope, when they read the stories!).

In my family, both characters are as well known as real members. My son sends me birthday cards signed "Dick

Henry," and we all discuss Dr. Cranston and Dick as though they were really living.

Our stories must have people to populate them; let's talk about short story characters. It makes no difference what kind of people they are; you must have characters to have a story. If you have animals, say, instead, you'll have to give them human characteristics to make the reader sympathetic to their situation.

A master like Hemingway molds a character who is completely believable to the reader. My students have finally concluded that there are only five ways a writer can make a "paper person" seem real, as in Hemingway's *The Old Man and the Sea.*

1. By expressing the true character of the person through his thoughts.
2. By his conversation—how and when he speaks.
3. By his reputation—what other people think of him.
4. By his appearance—what he looks like.
5. By his behavior—how he reacts to situations.

If you take the first letter of each of these five ways, you can form an acrostic: his thoughts, conversation, reputation, appearance, and behavior make the word T-crab.

T-houghts
C-onversation
R-eputation
A-ppearance
B-ehavior

Keep in mind this device. Using such a mnemonic device is helpful.

Are there other ways to make a pen-and-paper person seem real, to come alive? We haven't found any yet, for no matter who you are, real or fictitious, you are what you are because of your thoughts, your words, your reputation, your physical appearance, and your behavior.

Think it over. Is there another way to make a character stand up and appear real other than these five ways? Write and tell me if you find it. I'll add it to the list.

Let us discuss each of these ways authors use to create their "living" figures who move about in their stories. As we examine each of these methods, since characters are the first important essential of a short story, maybe some ideas may appeal to you to begin a story. Keep in mind those lines at the end of each chapter. Write down the ideas that occur to you as you read. They may be the start of another series as great as Sherlock Holmes' exploits with Dr. Watson. Who knows?

The thoughts of a person are an important index to his character. Think of Hamlet. He expresses aloud his thoughts in the famous soliloquy, the method used in Shakespeare's time to show what a character was thinking:

> I'll have these players
> Play something like the murder of my father
> Before mine uncle. I'll observe his looks;
> I'll tent him to the quick. If he but blench,
> I know my course. . .
> . . . .
> . . . The play's the thing
> Wherein I'll catch the conscience of the King.
>
> *(Hamlet, Act II, Scene II)*

From this we learn that Hamlet wants to try his uncle, to see whether he feels remorse or guilt when he views a play in which a monarch is slain. This scheme is to give Hamlet either confirmation of the ghost's message that his uncle has murdered Hamlet's father, or by seeming innocence on the uncle's part, an indication that the ghost was really a devil, tempting Hamlet to commit murder. So, the thought of a young man determined to put his uncle, the king, to the test, gives us an idea of the character of this wavering Shakespearean hero.

Let us assume in your story you have a student who stumbles upon a final test paper a day before the examination. He needs that subject to graduate, and he is weak in it. You write:

"As he stood there, holding the paper in his hands he couldn't believe his eyes."

Now you have a chance through his thoughts to show what kind of character this person is. Is he extremely honest? Is he dishonest? Is he an honest student, who now, however, finds himself tempted beyond his power to resist? You make the decision.

What does this indicate about the character:

"His eyes shone with delight. What a break! Now he could clobber that exam to a fare-thee-well! He'd not make it too good. Just about a 92 or so, to allay suspicion. But that was the break he wanted! A free ticket to graduation! He couldn't wait until he sat down to take the exam."

Or suppose you read this:

"Immediately he realized that he'd have to turn in the exam. That was the only thing to do. He had glimpsed part of it, so he would have to ask to be given a makeup test. He resolved, as he stood holding the paper, to go to the principal right away."

Yes, the thoughts of a character do indicate just what kind of a person he is. The description of a character's thinking goes a long way toward making the person seem real.

How a person speaks also shows us the kind of individual he is. If he massacres the King's English or uses hillbilly expressions, we get one idea. If he speaks with flawless phraseology, we get a different conception. If he stutters, or lisps, or always shouts, we learn something else about him.

What does the following opening paragraph from my short story "Sam Norton and the Little League" tell you about the speaker:

> "No, I won't cooperate! I think it's a crazy scheme, one of the most ridiculous I've ever heard of! And that's my final answer!"

Yes, Sam Norton, the "old codger" who speaks those words, is the "villain" of the story. He refuses to give land to enlarge the Little League field, to save the kids from running out into surrounding traffic. His opening words tell us quite a bit about him.

In stories years ago, dialect played a big part in indicating what part of the country or from what other nation a person came. Today editors seem to shy from printing dialect in short story conversation. Certainly, to write it is not easy, nor is it easy to read. My suggestion is, stay as far away from dialect as you can.

By the use of certain expressions, you can show something of the background of a person without using dialect.

> "I haven't had such fun since I was back on the farm in Minnesota," chortled Zeb as he climbed aboard a wooden horse on the merry-go-round.

Conversation is only one aspect of personality revealed. Use it to sketch the person but don't depend upon it to tell the reader what kind of person is speaking. Just as simple sentences have their place, and should not be overused, so conversation has its place.

In addition to a person's thoughts and words to reveal an individual, reputation indicates background. I shall never forget my experiences years ago seeing a stage version of the vampire thriller, "Dracula."

The play opened in a large drawing room in a London home. The characters on the stage were discussing the mysterious foreign gentleman who had recently moved into the mansion next door. He appeared to be suspiciously interested in things not usually spoken about. In the midst of the conversation, which also covered certain

crimes recently committed, with people found dead, their blood drained from their bodies, the butler entered.

"Count Dracula!" he announced, stepping aside to admit a tall, cloaked figure.

The entire audience, prepared for the entrance of this evil character, murmured an "Oh!" in such a unified manner that it sounded rehearsed. The Count's reputation had preceded him, and without his saying a single word, the audience felt it knew something about him.

Just as in a play minor characters talk about a major who will soon appear, so in a short story you can have people give their version of a man or woman's personality. "Oh, have you heard about ______?" the gossip runs, and by having the minor characters tell you something about the hero or heroine, or perhaps the villain, you learn more about him.

In my ice hockey story, "Penalty Hungry," which appeared in *Upward,* the narrator, one of the players on the team, tells the reader about the major character, Brad Morton.

> He had moved into the school district only a couple of weeks before we began practice. A big fellow, he was also a fast skater and a brilliant puck handler. He seemed the answer to our team's dream of a state championship.

What other characters think about and tell about a major character helps fill in the lines that make him true to life. Learn to make use of this third device, reputation, in our manufactured word "T-Crab."

Certainly a person's appearance tells a great deal about him. He is sloppy or "impeccably attired." He dresses "in

the height of fashion," or he "looks as though he'd slept in his clothes."

If his hair is always mussed, we form one conception of him. If he always wears black clothes or flashy clothes, or what-have-you, we form an idea of the person he is.

> Bud is pretty chubby, in fact looks something like a small-sized blimp.

What does that tell you about the hero of another yarn of mine? He isn't built like a Hollywood or TV matinee idol, rest assured.

In describing the physical appearance of characters, don't write reams and reams. Weave in the physical appearance from time to time. In fact in "Basketball Blimp," Bud in some places refers to his own appearance.

> Only a small miracle will ever get me on the varsity. Little guys just don't stand a chance anymore!

When the narrator tells little Bud that modern technology has done wonders, and men who have made great advances in the scientific world may offer hope to him, Bud says: "They can't make a 5′ 1″ shrimp tall or good enough to make a varsity basketball team, though!"

So the appearance of a character can be depicted by his own words, or those of another character, or by straight narration on the part of the author. Whichever manner you use, don't squeeze it all in at once. Keep the story moving as you delineate the people who are acting out their roles in it.

Finally, a person's behavior is a sure method of telling the reader what kind of a man or woman the story is about. After all, how a person acts under fire reveals character the most, as indicated in the mention of the student finding the final examination. What he finally decides to do and then actually does, tells us more about him than his words, his reputation, or his appearance.

Has a man conquered his temper or some evil aspect of his personality? It can be shown that he has or hasn't in the acts he performs. If he knocks down the person who criticizes him, then we know he still is a victim of his temper. If he clenches his fists, bites his lips, but refuses to punch the other character, we learn he is mastering self-control (Proverbs 16:32).

In the final analysis, during the climax of a story, when "the chips are down," we see by the protagonist's actions what he has become. It is an indication of whether he has changed or not, and it will be a barometer of what he will probably do in the future. His actions reveal his real character.

Review the five points of our little "T-Crab" device, and when you write try to use all aspects: the thoughts, conversation, reputation, appearance, and behavior of your characters. You will probably then have a well-rounded, well-developed literary figure, one your reader can accept as true-to-life.

Write a 300-400 word composition, utilizing as many of the five aspects of character-delineation found in "T-Crab" as you can naturally and smoothly. Don't be worried if you find at the end you've used only three or four. Within the compass of a briefer piece, you may not be able to do more. Wherever possible, begin to use all of these methods to make your characters seem realistic. You may use a real person in this composition or a fictitious one.

Characters are a vital part of any short story, but unless they are doing something, unless action is taking place, you have no tale. There must be a plot for a short story to take form. All the people or characters in the world jammed into a room, named and described in detail, will not constitute a short story. They must be involved in action with each other or within themselves.

Basically, as you may remember from your study of

literature, there are three forms of conflict, the foundation of all stories:

1. Man against man
2. Man against nature
3. Man against himself

Every short story worthy of the name recites the conflict a main character has either with another person or persons, his environment, or within himself. Most of the time, two struggles, two conflicts go on, as in the case of a man struggling across the burning desert who has to keep telling himself to persevere. He is struggling both against the forces of nature and the inner forces within himself.

In the first type of plot a man opposes some other person or group. This may also involve two groups, as two teams, or two political parties, or two bands of people (cowboys and Indians, if you will). Nevertheless, it is human beings against human beings.

Both want the same thing—land, money, fame, or victory of some sort. In their head-on collision to secure their ends, they create the suspense and action called the plot, the episodes that make up the story. The telling of this struggle, with its conclusion in doubt, is, in effect, the short story.

In an elementary sense, therefore, the plot is the battle between two forces. Narrowed down to a definite background, it might be a simple but dramatic story such as Jack London's "To Build a Fire." Here a man struggles in the frozen wastes of the Yukon simply to survive. He battles against the forces of nature, finally succumbing.

In contrast to most stories which end happily, here the forces of nature win out. But the fact remains that a struggle went on; the recital of that conflict made the story. A character faced a problem, a struggle, and had to do something about it.

It makes little difference which of the three conflicts you choose as the basis of plot; you will have to decide which

of the three will be the main one. Will the accent be on the outer, external struggle, against other people or nature's forces, or will it be the inner struggle? You will concentrate on the conflict you wish to dramatize, perhaps using another secondary conflict to augment it.

The conflicts between people can be on a personal level, such as two men wanting the same girl or the same public office or to make the varsity, or on a group basis, such as two teams vying against each other or two armies fighting. In most short stories, it is best to stay with a single individual, even if he is part of a larger group. A solitary player who has a problem, even if it is sketched against the background of the whole team and school, is far more effective. Read the dramatic story of Esther in the Bible book bearing her name.

In a short story you have only so many words; you are limited in your space to tell the tale. You can't waste words or use them lavishly, as in a novel. You have to get in as much as you can of plot, characterization, and background within the given space. It is therefore much more effective to concentrate on the single personality.

Here is a short story plot submitted by a student. Do you feel you could do anything with this sketchy outline?

> A girl is invited to a college football weekend, complete with dinner dance, but at the same time she knows she should be studying for a very important Monday examination. She is a high school senior, and although she is interested in accepting the invitation to leave Friday afternoon to go to the distant college town for the long weekend, which will probably bring her back home late Sunday night, she wonders about missing out on the studying. What should she do?

Now this is a realistic individual problem that a typical high school girl today might face. Within the compass of, say, 1,500 words or so, the space allotted to such stories in many youth weeklies, you cannot use too many words to develop the plot or the characterization. You can describe the girl and her problem, then show, in the development of the story proper, just what she decides to do about it all.

In this story you can't go into descriptions of the entire football game, the opposing teams, the backgrounds of the high school girl and her escort. You have to concentrate on one character and her struggle, which, in this case, is an inner one. In reality this is a "man against himself" struggle.

In the short stories of today, limit yourself to one character involved in a situation, and you will write more effectively. You will be able to make this character seem true-to-life, using the various characterization devices symbolized by our coined word "T-Crab," and you will be able to write a dramatic yarn. You will not splash words all over the landscape, covering a variety of scenes inadequately, but you will utilize a few effectively.

The plotting of your story, whether of inner or external conflict, will have a beginning, a development, and a climax. The climax is the most exciting moment of the story, when the game is won or lost, the murderer unmasked. The story logically ends a few sentences later. After this most dramatic moment, say, when the winning basket is scored and the gym explodes with the victory roar of the spectators, bring your story to a quick conclusion.

The number of scenes or episodes you use to tell your story depends upon the length of your tale. If a story can only be 1,500 words, you don't have too much opportunity to move your protagonist from place to place. Maybe only two or three actual episodes are possible. Be guided accordingly.

Remember, too, as you may have noticed in good stories you have read, to start your story as close as possible to the most exciting point. This creates interest and suspense. Some of the great writers also believe you should keep the actual time occurring in the story as close as possible to the time it takes to read it.

This is not easy. If it takes fifteen minutes to read a short story, is this all the time it should take for the fictional character to act? Yes, according to these experts. It means that you will take the most dramatic fifteen minutes of the incident to focus attention just on this action, thus squeezing all your drama into this short span of time.

By means of a flashback you can review what led up to the climax, you can paint in the necessary details to show the importance of the suspenseful moments.

Let's illustrate. You have a basketball player who gets panicky when he comes to shoot foul shots in a tight game. You therefore start your story near the point where he is going to have to face this problem in an important game, the most important one of the season.

The game is on, but you inform the reader, quickly, in a flashback, what makes this a nerve-wracking experience for Bob. The game is seesawing back and forth. A point or two might mean the county championship.

Only ten minutes are left to play when you start the story and lead up to Bob's having to toss in a pair of fouls. As he races up and down the court, you are in the mind of Bob, you flash back to his experiences in other games when he botched up the situation.

> He remembered that time he had caused the Bellport game to go into overtime when he flubbed a foul shot. Give him the ball at midcourt and let him dribble down and he'd usually make the shot. But that foul!

Within the space of your short story, you concentrate, from a chronological standpoint, on only ten minutes, the time it might take for someone to read your story. And if you do, it makes the story more realistic, more dramatic.

The time problem is worth considering further. Let us suppose you are going to write a story about a man whose child has been kidnaped. The kidnapers inform him he has a certain time to get the $10,000 or his child will disappear forever.

You have the short space of say six or seven typewritten pages within which you must show the mental agony of the father, his concern for his child, and what he finally attempts in an effort to save his baby. Will you write that the kidnapers gave him six months to get the money, one month, or forty-eight hours?

Will you have a dramatic, suspenseful tale if you spread your story thin over a six months period, or compress it all into a very much shorter period? The answer is obvious. The briefer the time your short story embraces, the more realistic and effective it will be.

Where do plots for short stories come from? There are several answers, one of which might be more congenial to one writer than another.

One author says he somehow begins to envision an unusual character, then with the personality vivid, places him in a predicament in which he has to act. Another author begins to think of a situation, a plot puzzle, and then creates characters to fit into it. A third author says he sees some minor, trivial object, lets his imagination start working, and puts a character into a situation using that object. It is said that Jack London developed "To Build a Fire" from seeing a man use up his last match attempting to get some wood burning.

Some authors start with background, and place their fictional people up against it and let them act. Still others want to tell a lesson, point out some universal, eternal truth. They select characters, background and plot and mold them all together to get across their point.

In her book *How to Write a Story and Sell It,* Adela Rogers St. John, Hollywood scenarist and short story writer, warns against taking any incident a real person tells you and simply retelling it. In the first place it isn't fiction, and in the second it may not sound as dramatic retold on paper.

But this does not mean that the germ of a short story cannot be a real life incident. We have mentioned that a short item in the *New York Times* about men climbing a mountain was the inspiration for "Mountain Peril."

You must reweave the true life incident, embellish it, make it more dramatic, if you are to use it as the basis of a story. This is where your story-telling ability comes to the fore. Can you take a simple, one paragraph item from a daily paper and rework it into an intensely gripping yarn that the reader can't put down?

Don't be afraid to look for unusual events, or even some that are not unusual but simply interest you. Make a note to try to develop them into a full-length short story. It might be as simple as a girl friend confiding in you that she doesn't know whether or not she should be a nurse.

Another word of caution: stick to the believable, average people, facing situations we all face, if you ever want to get your stories published. What have been called "off-trail" stories don't permit the readers to "identify" with the main characters, a "must" for most editors.

In this regard, Georges Polti has written a book, *The Thirty-Six Dramatic Situations,* in which he suggests that all stories are a variation of one of these basic plot outlines. It is worth studying.

You have your characters and your plot. They have to get together somewhere, sometime. The time and place of the story is called the background, or setting. The story cannot take place in a vacuum.

It makes no difference where you decide to set the story, as long as you can paint in the background to make the

tale plausible. It is a good idea to write only about backgrounds with which you are personally familiar.

On the other hand, James Hilton, who wrote *Lost Horizon,* a story of a lost land in Tibet where no one ever grew old or unhappy, admitted he got all his information from the *National Geographic* magazine! Reading can give you knowledge of other places and times, enabling you to write with authority and conviction. In fact, the more popular authors read and research all the time to gain authenticity.

All of these essentials to a good short story—realistic, sympathetic characters, a plot which moves along swiftly, credibly, an appropriate background—must be interwoven. You don't write a full paragraph about the background, then move to the description of a character for another paragraph, then to the plot.

In short stories, the three aspects of characterization, plot, and background merge. They appear in the same paragraph, keep the story moving. Here's a paragraph from my short story "High Tension," published in *The Christian,* later reprinted in *The Link,* a magazine chaplains distribute to the armed services:

> Jeff Hudson held tightly to the inside handle of the door as the utility truck slowly turned onto the main highway out of town. As the power company vehicle hit the smooth, treacherous sleet of the road, the truck skidded, almost landing in the ditch.

In this paragraph we have our main character mentioned, something of the background sketched for us, and the story begun, a merging of the three phases of the story: character, plot, and background.

Most short stories, though this is not always immediately apparent, contain a lesson: Honesty is the Best Policy, Perseverance Pays, Learn to Obey Orders. You can go on and write some of your own. In fact, most stories, though they appear to have been written simply for the sake of entertainment, usually have a moral, "sugar-coated" perhaps, but there.

In our Creative Writing classes each student is asked to select the field of fiction or non-fiction (the short story or article-essay), then write a 1,500 word paper. The short story or article is submitted to a magazine. Our class motto is: "A check or a rejection slip." We feel it is all good experience for the young writer.

Why not resolve to write a short story and submit it to one of the juvenile house publishers listed at the end of this book? You may begin a professional writing career. Whether or not you get your first piece accepted, the experience is valuable for anyone who desires to become a writer.

A final suggestion. Read some of the great short stories of the past, notably those of Poe, Hawthorne, Benet, and Faulkner. They will inspire and entertain you. And keep reading whatever you can find on the short story. Become a keen student of the art of weaving a make-believe incident so that your reader "suspends his disbelief" and accepts it for the moment as real.

Write the first 300-400 words of a short story based on

1. an item in the newspaper
2. an incident you heard of from real life
3. an unusual character you have created
4. a house, car, or other thing which you have seen recently

Introduce your main character in the first 150 words and set the plot going. Give him some sort of problem he has to solve. At a later date you may want to finish this opening, perhaps after consultation with your instructor.

Have any new ideas occurred to you while reading this chapter? Write them down to expand later when you are searching for ideas:

The Article

Chapter 6

". . .and out of Zebulun they that handle the pen of the writer" *(Judges 5:14).*

When I began a writing career years ago, short stories were the vogue. Most magazines featured three times as much fiction as essays or articles, or what has come to be called "non-fiction." The larger magazines had as many as seven or eight short stories and only one or two articles.

This proportion has been completely reversed. Although short stories continue to entertain millions, most periodicals today feature articles. Apparently life is moving at such a rapid, dramatic pace that "truth is [indeed] stranger than fiction." Who can write a short story any more thrilling than an astronaut's experience in space?

Today I still write short stories, but my major effort is on articles. They are what editors seem to want most.

An "article" is any piece of non-fiction from, say, 500 to 5,000 words. The article may be a two-page (typewritten) bit on Seattle's Christmas Ship, which I wrote for *Teens,* or a longer 2,000 word feature, complete with photos, such as "Nathan Hale's Heritage," which ran in *New York State Education.* The lengths vary; some articles have photos, some do not; subjects are usual and unusual, but they have one thing in common: they are true, factual pieces.

Years ago the term "essay" was used to describe such

magazine features. It meant an attempt (an essay, or try) by the author, usually an erudite, scholarly individual who had traveled extensively, to describe his visit to Ethiopia, or to detail some theory he had about economics or science. The style was usually pedantic, and did not always interest the average reader.

As the years went on, however, magazine editors began to revise pieces, making them more interesting to the man in the street, selecting topics that might interest him. Today, pick up a magazine and you find an article on any conceivable subject under the sun. Such a monthly as *Reader's Digest* is made up of articles of every kind. In fact, that is how that periodical began, as a digest of "one article a day" for each month. Occasionally, today, a short story slips in.

In a previous chapter we have given you some hints how to find ideas for articles. Refresh your memory by rereading Chapter Three. Use some of these methods to jog your own mind. Be on the alert for subjects to write about. And keep reading, to see what is being published.

It has been said that the definition of a noun also describes a magazine article: "A person, place or thing." I have written about such persons as Van Cliburn, the youthful Christian American who went to Moscow and won the Tschaikovsky piano concert competition, and Bob Richards, the young preacher-athlete who became an Olympic star. I have written about President James A. Garfield, the only preacher to become Chief Executive; Frank Laubach, who has taught six million people to read; and J.C. Penney, the American merchant prince.

I have met only a few of these people personally. Most of the people I write about I have never seen face to face. To write a factual article about them, I have had to do research.

So let's talk about research, backbone of the modern article. You are familiar with some aspects of research, or should be, by the time you take this book in your hand.

An article writer makes use of every research source. He reads articles mentioned in the library's *Reader's Guide to Periodical Literature,* articles which reveal much about the latest activities of a person he may be writing about. Perhaps he learns more from *Current Biography,* a "must" for all article writers.

Armed with the latest published material, he often tries to add newer facts by corresponding with the subject of the article, or by newspaper reference. The latter is not always the best, for often people who are worth articles are not the ones who get their names splashed across the front page.

Sometimes you may be able to interview the person. At a church meeting in Chicago, I telephoned Dr. Henry H. Halley, the great, great, great grandnephew of the discoverer of "Halley's Comet." The doctor had written a remarkable book, a Bible handbook. It had started as a sixteen-page booklet, grown to 32, then 64, then 128 pages, and when I last heard, was a volume of almost 1,000 pages, in its 23rd edition!

Dr. Halley very graciously suggested I come right up. We had an enjoyable time, during which he gave me a good idea of his background, a photograph, and a copy of the latest edition of his handbook. I sat and made notes of all he told me.

Since, I have written two versions of the story behind his unusual book, concentrating in one case on the book and the other, the way it came to be written.

With regard to taking notes during a personal interview, let me suggest that it is best not to start writing at once. Taking out a pad or a piece of paper often distracts people. It makes them "freeze," and they don't give as full an interview as they might.

It has been suggested that the proper way to start an interview is to sit down and become interested in whatever the other person introduces. By having done some advance research you know some of the things he has done, so you might suggest some light topic, one which he will be glad to discuss with you, particularly if it bears on something commendable he has done.

After chatting a while, you might say, "That's an interesting point; I'd like to write it down." Now take out your piece of paper and jot some notes. Most experienced writers suggest it be on a single piece of typewriter paper, folded several times to fit inconspicuously in the palm of the hand.

I fold a sheet in half, then in threes, so that I have six small sections to write on, using always only one side. This sixth of a sheet fits nicely in the palm of the hand.

When interviewing someone, don't be afraid to ask whether he has a photograph, or some clippings, or brochures, or any other printed materials. Tell him you will ask the editor to return the photo if it is published, after the "cut" is made and that, after you have thoroughly reviewed the printed matter, you will yourself return that. Often the person will tell you to keep the picture or the materials, but sometimes he will want them all returned. Keep faith with him.

I usually tell those interviewed that I will see they receive a copy of the article if it is printed, and I try to do it, too, since most publications furnish either tearsheets (the article torn out of the periodical) or complete copies of the magazine.

Thank the person for his time. Learn how to close an interview properly. Don't stand lingering at the door for fifteen minutes, but get up and leave. You might, as a parting remark, state that it might be necessary to check some information in the future, and you might write or phone for it. Your subject will usually be more than willing to help you.

All of this applies to the personal interview, something not always possible. You are not in Chicago, San Francisco, Des Moines, or Detroit. Does that mean you have to depend only on the material you find in magazines, old material? By no means.

Most of my "interviewing" takes place by correspondence. In this way I learn about my subject's latest activities and accomplishments, which are not in *Current Biography* or some other periodical. A letter from Bob Richards on the West Coast to me on the East, informed me that he has started a company to make motion pictures for teenagers. I didn't find this in any current periodical. I added it to my article and this information updated my piece.

Interviewing by correspondence is fairly simple.

After I learn of a person I wish to write about, I write him an introductory letter, something like this:

> Dear Mr. Handel:
>
> Some time ago I learned that although you are not related to the composer, George Frederick Handel, you have made a hobby of collecting unusual anecdotes about this great musician. Since I would like to write an article about your unusual hobby, I wonder whether you would be kind enough to fill out the enclosed questionnaire. Also, I would appreciate it if you could forward me a glossy photograph of yourself and any clippings or other material about your hobby, which I would be happy to return to you after perusal.
>
> If the article is accepted for publication I will ask the editor to return your photo to you after the "cut" is made.
>
> I am a free lance writer who has written for many youth, church, travel, and hobby periodicals, and if the article is printed, will be happy to forward you a copy for your files.
>
> With all best wishes,
>
> Sincerely,
>
> William Folprecht
>
> William Folprecht

The form of the questionnaire varies somewhat, depending upon the nature of the hobby, occupation, or unusual aspect of the subject's life I am covering in the article. But generally I write something like this, on a regular 8½ x 11″ bond sheet:

QUESTIONNAIRE TO MR. FRANK G. HANDEL

Full name ______________________________

Birthplace and date ______________________________

Early schooling ______________________________

Later education ______________________________

Name of parents and birthplaces ______________________________

Part they played in early development ______________________________

How and when you started your hobby ______________________________

____

____

Any unusual aspects (incidents, discoveries) while pursuing

hobby ______________________________

____

Amount of material currently accumulated ______________________________

____

Anything else of interest ______________________________

____

Often the person fills this out, adds a few notes on the back, or sends an accompanying letter with it. Sometimes he does not complete the questionnaire, but writes a lengthy letter giving all the necessary details of his hobby or work. Some of the people I have written have sent a wealth of material, as did an Oklahoma college professor renowned for his reading of Charles Dickens' *A Christmas Carol.* This man, who had started reciting snatches of the famous story during the war while his buddies and he waited for enemy action, had resumed his hobby when peace came, and had made a name for himself throughout the West and Southwest, traveling to churches, schools, colleges, and town halls to entertain crowds.

Professor Earl W. Oberg sent me newspaper clippings, other magazine articles, a photo of himself, both in costume and regular college classroom garb, along with a fully completed questionnaire and an accompanying letter. I, of course, returned all the information after I had thoroughly digested it before writing an article published by *The Lookout.* In addition, I requested the editor to return the photo to Professor Oberg.

The published article was more interesting, I believe, because of these added materials, but the questionnaire starts the ball rolling, and even if no printed pieces accompany it, can still give a great deal of information.

In a few cases I have not had a response to my introductory letter; in most cases my "subject" has responded within a reasonable length of time and has furnished me with materials needed.

People usually form the subject matter of articles, whether the articles are specifically about their hobbies, their lifework, or their ambitions. Be alert to the unusual folks who may live around you, or who may go to the same school. Often there is a teacher on your faculty who has had some unusual experiences or done something out of the ordinary—studied in a remote region, served as a missionary, or perhaps climbed the Matterhorn as a hobby.

While we have been discussing articles for paid publication, remember our advice, don't always think of writing for money alone. You might be able to write a fascinating article for your school paper about a teacher or fellow student in the form of a feature article. You might write a piece for your town newspaper.

Without characters, no short story is real. Without people doing something, as a rule, there is no article. Just as the definition of a noun uses the word "person" first (a noun is the name of a person, place or thing), so in articles people, individuals are the most important.

In any effort to write feature articles for the school newspaper, use some of the interview techniques mentioned. Make an appointment, keep your note paper out of the way so your subject does not "freeze," and be grateful and gracious.

Our school newspaper, *The Thunderbird,* has begun a feature series known as "Teacher of the Issue." In this piece the student reporter develops a teacher's unusual qualities, educational background, and experiences. The feature has become one of the most popular ever run.

Awareness of the lives of people we see every day, whether teachers, fellow students, friends, neighbors, or relatives, can lead to great discoveries. I was in a rest home for the aged where everyone was excited over the fact that a very active "guest" had just celebrated his 100th birthday.

It was quite an event, no doubt, but in talking with another man, fifteen years younger, I learned that the 85-year-old man had had some incredible experiences years ago in the United States Navy.

Just as a small coin held up in front of our eye can blot out all the beauty of the landscape, so often we fail to see the unusual, the strange, the interesting right in front of us.

Be on your guard lest you miss interesting people all around you! If they will permit, learn their story, and write it up.

Since you are now in the non-fiction field, what you write must be based on truth, must be factual. Although you may use some "dedicated imagination" when writing non-fiction, you may never twist facts to suit your purpose. So write factually on one of the following, or on some person of interest, preparing a well-organized 300-400 word composition:

"My Friend's Unusual Hobby"
"A Student from Across the Seas"
"A Teacher with an Unusual Background"
"How to Interview"
"A Historical Personality I Wish I Had Met"
"Baseball's Weirdest Character" (or Greatest Hitter, Pitcher, or Fielder)

Modern transportation has opened wide a door for Americans. By plane, train, ship, and car we travel all over our own mainland and the world. As we journey, we are

fascinated with the old and the new, the bizarre and the ordinary.

We seek information about places we might visit ourselves sometime, as well as those we may never get to. Articles about places near and far, domestic and foreign, attract us.

This is an opportunity for the creative writer—to describe places he himself has visited or heard about. Even if he has not actually been there, the imaginative, diligent writer can research a spot from a distance and describe it to the satisfaction of editor and reader. I have done it myself, so I know it is possible.

Firsthand information is the most effective. If you have actually been to a place, you can do a better job of describing it than if you've only read about it. Three summers spent at beautiful Lake Chautauqua, with its music, plays, lectures, meetings, and church services in a 7,000-seat amphitheater, enabled me to write about it in a five-page illustrated piece run by *Travel* magazine.

On the other hand, I had never been to Clifton's Cafeteria in Los Angeles, yet I wrote "Garden of Influence," published by *Sunday Digest*.

When one seeks information about places he has not personally visited, he uses somewhat the same method as he does for persons. Let us assume you have heard of an unusual Indian reservation, and you want to write about it. There appears to be little or no current information on it. You do know it is located somewhere in or near a certain city, say, in Oklahoma.

Write a gracious letter to the Reservation, explaining that you would like to know more about it for an article you are hoping to write. Ask for any literature, clippings, or other materials available. Sometimes you may receive the answer that material is available for a price. In that case, if you truly desire to write the piece, you will have to forward the money.

In many cases, however, I have found that the request for material that may bring added fame, honor, glory to the area, results in all the free material I can use. If the area is one which will really benefit from publicity, the people in charge, such as a chamber of commerce manager, will be very happy to send along all the material available, usually telling you to keep it.

Sometimes, too, they have glossy photos to lend or to give you to illustrate the article. Remember, when you submit photos, be sure they are "glossies." Publishers can use just about any size, but they usually prefer 5″ x 7″ or 8″ x 10″ shots.

In writing to an area, you will, of course, tell them that if your article is published, you will send them a copy. This is nothing more than common courtesy. Make a habit of telling them this, and then doing it.

On occasion, you may be able to telephone for information. I did this to get the facts for "Youth Hall of Fame," published by *Futures,* a monthly periodical published by the Junior Chamber of Commerce in Oklahoma. The man who was the originator of the Hall lived in Pennsylvania, and I decided to call him for information and possible pictures. He gave me the needed information over the telephone.

After getting information, you must digest it thoroughly. Read it several times to "get the flavor." Rough out notes. Often some new thought will occur to you as you read, and you'll discover that the information is not in the material.

This may necessitate another letter. Simply write and advise that you have read all the material, and would like to know about a few more items. There doesn't seem to be mention of such and such a person in the latter part of the material, for example, although he is described earlier. Or you might want more up-to-date material, the brochure you now have only going up to, say, ten years ago. Write and request more complete data.

As you finally begin to write your piece, make some more rough notes. Spend a great deal of time on the title and the opening. An editor will spot these first. A good title and a good beginning may intrigue him to read further. It will also be of help to you; you will know in what direction to move as you write.

Perhaps you will tackle the article from a chronological viewpoint, or take another approach. Try several approaches in an effort to see which sounds the best to you. Many professional authors write and rewrite an opening six or seven times, then judge which is the best.

The research is vital to the success of the piece. It is claimed that although only ten percent of the research proper (the facts you have accumulated) appears in the finished version, something like an iceberg with the greater section "underwater," nevertheless the importance of having done far more than shows in the article will be apparent to an editor and to readers.

A shallow article is one in which it is evident you are stretching information. After all, if you do not have enough to write a full article, you can go back and do more research, or simply write the piece as a "filler."

Fillers are very brief, usually not more than 500 word pieces which some magazines like to use to fill up pages. A longer story or article ends, let us say, about halfway down a page. The filler neatly completes the page.

Lloyd Derrickson, who used to write short stories for a Cincinnati weekly on which I was youth editor, wrote an article in a professional writer's journal: "Want a Check? Write a Filler!" Often this is one of the quickest ways to get money, since some of the modern magazines seem to want more and more of these and are paying for them, witness *Reader's Digest*.

But let's get back to the full-length article, one that you have sufficiently researched. You have all the material, as much as you will need, and more. You must arrange it. How will you go about it?

If you will remember some of the "stunts" you may have pulled while writing a long term paper, it will be helpful. The magazine writer doesn't pull his long publishable article out of his magic hat. He uses the very same methods a student does in preparing a term paper. In fact, years ago I took a term paper I had to write at Teachers' College, rewrote it a bit and sold it!

Some people use 3 x 5 cards to put their information on. Others use sheets of paper, large or small. Just don't write on both sides. When you place these cards or sheets down, you want to be able to scan them all to see where you should start. You may have something important on the reverse side of a sheet, if you are foolish enough to write on both sides, and may forget to use it at all.

Place the notes in the order you decide is proper. As you start writing, simply place the used note to one side and go on to the next. Simple as it sounds, this is the way to utilize your data.

If you can, intersperse your factual material with incidents or dialogue. Keep the "story" moving. Use these devices to illuminate the facts. The piece is not merely a factual one. You aren't writing an item for the encyclopedia. You are engaged in "creative writing." Entertain, teach, instruct, inspire, guide.

What places can you write about? Almost every place. Keep your ears open to hear of interesting places, maybe out of the passing conversation of visiting Aunt Minnie or Uncle Edgar you'll get an idea. "Saw a most remarkable cabin in Ohio last summer on our vacation," Uncle Edgar says, while you're sitting around the barbecue. Your ears prick up.

What kind was it? Why was it remarkable? If you are interested, write for the information. You may be on the way to a good article.

Pen magazine carried my article, "America's Lilliput," about a tiny, model-railroad-scaled diorama built by a man in Pennsylvania. *The War Cry,* Salvation Army magazine, ran my piece, "Monument to a Mother." It described the huge Cadle Tabernacle in Indianapolis, built in honor of an evangelist's mother. *Upward* published an article I'd written on "Museum for Americans," about the Dearborn, Michigan museum. *Twelve/Fifteen,* the Methodist youth weekly, printed "America's Soaring Capital," in which I described Harris Hill, in Elmira, where motorless aircraft are pulled to the edge of the mountain by a truck or car, then soar over the valley below.

People are interested in reading of all kinds of places.

Maybe something you know about some place that you take for granted, will be completely new to others.

Never underestimate people's desire for knowledge. They want to learn of new places, even if they can never go there in person. And you, too, will be inspired by the vicarious journeys you yourself take by writing for information.

People - Places - Things. If you are a creative writer writing about life today and yesterday, you can certainly write about "things" such as sports, religion, school, home life, just about anything.

The market is always good for sports articles. I have written about hockey, baseball, lacrosse, basketball and football. Get your information from firsthand viewing or participation.

I'm an old basketball player myself. Not as old as the inventor of the sport, as some of my more ebullient students suggest when I mention I played the old "cage game," but I did play actively for seven years.

My playing knowledge was augmented by reading, and then by a trip to Springfield, Massachusetts, where Dr. James Naismith actually invented the sport eighty-five years or so ago. I've written about the "Sport That Was Invented" and the articles were run by several youth magazines, separated by the span of a decade, for I wrote two versions, each stressing a different aspect of the game.

In writing a lacrosse piece, I used my knowledge as a spectator, as a reader, and as a friend of the coach of our high school team.

You can write about anything under the sun which interests you, and you will always do a much better job if you are interested. If it's a sport, you don't have to have played it, but you will have to be interested enough in it so that even if some of the facts you find yourself gathering don't at the moment seem gripping or world-shattering, you will continue for the sake of your general interest in the subject.

You can write about such things as the Pledge of Allegiance. *Straight* magazine published my version of the story behind this pledge. In a similar vein, I wrote about the Christian flag, and naming it "Flag of Faith," sent it to *Steps,* a young people's weekly, which ran it.

When our Sunday School in Pennsylvania decided to have its own newspaper, I wrote about that, in an article called "Read All About It!" The David C. Cook Publishing Company in Elgin, Illinois, printed it so that other schools might consider duplicating our efforts.

Magazines today are looking for "How-To" articles. I once wrote "How to Make a Bible Museum," a summer camp project for churches and Sunday schools. This came right from my memory, as I recalled a minister who long ago had initiated one.

Sports car repairs, how to make a new cake, suggestions for improving one's personality, appearance, reading habits, or even how to train your new puppy, all may find a home in a periodical's pages. The trick is to gather the information, prepare it in an interesting fashion, find a place where something like it has not been run recently, and send it in.

The How-To articles are horses of a different color from non-fiction pieces about persons and places. They must be firsthand experiences, with directions that work. You must have done the "How-To" yourself, or at least watched someone else do it. If you write a How-To article, make sure you are on solid ground.

Remember that although people are interested in other people, and in places, and in things, they are also interested in themselves. The self-improvement article is in great demand.

Although many of them are written by experts in the

field of psychiatry, education, religion, and science, and the larger magazines will accept such pieces only from such professionals, many teen-age magazines look for personal experience pieces from people the same age as their readers, or slightly older.

"How We Conduct Our Young People's Meetings" might sell to a youth magazine that wants to learn of new ideas to interest the youth of its denomination. "Try This on Your Record Player" might be an article for a youth magazine looking for hints from its own readers. "Our School Does It This Way" might be the title of an interesting one-shot article or series for a magazine interested in American youth and its pursuits.

Once again: Be careful of humor. You may want to poke fun at yourself and your contemporaries, but walk warily along the humor road. You can find more salable material in the serious or semi-serious.

And be persistent in not only looking for new ideas of things you can write about, but in writing about them and revising them. If you think them good enough to send out for editorial scrutiny, don't hide your light under a bushel, send them out! Manuscripts hidden in your desk do not bring in editorial notes or checks.

When an acquaintance started talking to me about her writing, saying she had written quite a bit, I asked, "Has any of it been published?"

"Oh, no," she said, "I've never shown it to anyone!"

Good luck to her. Maybe one of the greatest literary finds of the century will occur when all of those dusty scripts are unearthed after she passes on.

For the truly creative writer, such modesty is silly. You have created something. You should want others to share it with you, like a beautiful painting, or a piece of music.

If you think it's the best you can do, send it out. It may bring home a rejection slip. That's just one less before you find yourself published!

Write a 300-400 word composition (which might be the beginning of a longer piece) on one of the following, or on some topic you'd like to write about:

> "How My Favorite Sport Originated"
> "A Museum I Visited Recently"
> "An Unusual Program My Youth Group Enjoyed"
> "My School's Greatest Honor"

Any new ideas for writing occur to you while reading this chapter? Write them down here for future writing:

Chapter 7

The Manuscript and Its Market

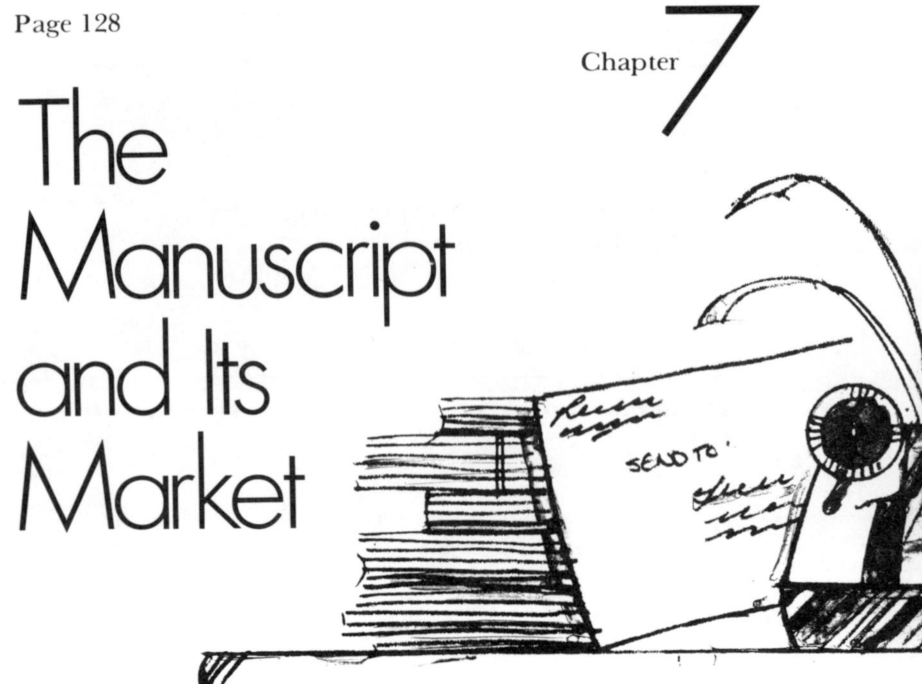

"And the word of the Lord was published throughout all the region" *(Acts 13:49)*.

One of the pleasant aspects of the writer's trade is that the editor who receives your manuscript does not care about your age or your looks or anything else of that nature. All he wants to know is, do you write correctly and interestingly? Do you create material that will help him fill the pages of his periodical?

As an editor in Ohio, I had little opportunity to learn what most of my contributors looked like, and I didn't care. I wanted good stories, articles, serials, and fillers for the pages it was my job to make up each week.

At one time, I asked regular contributors to send me a capsule biography and a photo to run. This gave our readers (and me) a chance to see what the writers looked

like, but physical appearance had nothing to do with what I accepted or rejected.

Most of the time no note needs to accompany your story or article. Let the piece stand or fall on its own merit. (If you write an absorbing article or an interesting piece of fiction, the editor may write for information about you, and he may not.)

You must make your script, then, acceptable in all ways, both from the mechanical (the outward, external) standpoint and the literary (the inner, or content).

Resolve always to hand in professional looking material. Be a "pro" from the beginning.

This means neat typing, a minimum of technical errors

(which you can remedy as inconspicuously as possible), and the correct form. Depending upon what "market" you are after, this form will vary.

For the average magazine, the general format is as follows:

On your first sheet, type your name and address in the upper left hand corner, one inch down and an inch in from the left edge. Across the page, in the right hand corner, type the number of words, one inch down and one inch from the right. Some writers type immediately below this "First serial rights only."

This statement means that the periodical is being offered the right to publish the story or article one time, and then, if the author so desires he may retype it and send it out to another magazine, some time after the first one has printed it. The second time a published piece is mailed out, he must advise the editor that this was first published in such and such a magazine on such and such a date and he is now offering "second rights."

Some of the publications I have written for have accepted my manuscript on the first rights basis and published it, sending along a check either upon acceptance or publication. At a later date, if I feel I want to send it out on a second rights basis to some other periodical, I do so, advising them that this already has been published once.

Ethically and legally, until it has been published, you have no right to send out again a piece you have already sold first rights on. There may be exceptions to the rule, say, in the case of a magazine which bought it and went out of business. Even then, another publication might have bought the magazine's assets and has the right to use the article first. By and large, for any reprint, it's best to wait until it will be just that, a reprinted piece.

In the juvenile and religious field I have had some unusual experiences. The Methodist Church publishing house, in Nashville, now purchases all rights, which means that if it desires to reprint articles or sell them, it may. One time the company did that to my work and sent me a percentage of the reprint sale.

I sold a sports story to the Westminster Press, in Philadelphia. Although I had indicated "first serial rights," the form which accompanied the check indicated that I was selling all rights, but that if the purchaser sold it on a reprint basis, I would receive 50% of the reprint sale.

I cite these cases, just to give you some idea of the different ways publishers may operate. Most of the larger magazines purchase all rights, but after they have published, will release other rights to you, as the author, upon your personal, written request.

One religious publishing house I have written for will pay 2¢ per word if you sell all rights and 1¢ a word if you sell first serial only.

Other experiences which have gladdened my heart included a letter from an editor advising that he had read my story in another periodical and wanted to reprint it. He offered a sum for the reprint rights that was more than I'd been paid originally. If the reprint magazine has a larger circulation, this may well happen.

This matter of rights you see can become a little confusing. Many authors merely put the approximate number of words in the right-hand corner.

Incidentally, sometimes I also type a third line at the top of the first page for articles: "Pix on Request." If I have good, glossy shots to illustrate my piece, lacrosse or basketball photos, let us say, I want the editor to know it, but I save a great deal of postage by not enclosing the photos. If he is interested in the article, he will ask to see the pictures.

After you have typed the information at the top of your paper, skip about three inches and type your title in capitals (centered). After that skip two lines and center "by" the name you want to accompany the published piece.

You may use a name other than your own, a pen name, but like most authors, you will want the name that appears on check and by-line to be your own name.

Skip two lines and start your story or article, double spacing it all through. Leave at least a one inch margin all around the script, typed on 8½ x 11″ white bond typewriter paper. Make sure you type a carbon copy for yourself.

Your first page, then, will look something like this:

Professional writers do not usually count each word, but count only the number of lines on a page, then take three or four individual lines to get the average. If you have 25 lines on a sheet, with about ten words average (which you strike by taking the total actual number of words on three lines, for example), you can estimate you average 250 words on a page. Four pages give you a total of 1,000 words.

This matter of approximation of wordage is a guide to the editor in considering your script. When you learn that a certain paper will only run 1,500 word stories and articles up to 1,000, don't send that outfit 2,500 word stories or 1,500 word articles. In almost every instance, it will

send material back, often without even taking the trouble to read it.

Be professional, acquaint the busy editor with the number of words in your creation. This will also help him make out the check, too, since many magazines pay so much per word.

We have discussed page one. What about the succeeding pages?

Well, some writers type their name and the page number in the upper right corner of each page starting with page two. Some writers type the name of the story or article and then the page number.

Whether you type "Jones - 2," or "Happy Days at Camp - 2" on your succeeding pages sometimes depends upon the publishers you are writing for. In sheets of instruction which they often send out to prospective contributors, some publishers indicate just what they would like you to do for name or title identification.

From page two on, start about an inch or so from the top and make sure you have an inch all around. We repeat: Although your first page has a longer, three-inch space before you start the title and story, you start typing one inch down and one inch in on page two and succeeding pages.

Don't ever staple the pages of your manuscript, or use pins or paper clips. Keep them loose, neat, easily accessible.

Your story or article may finish on page four or five, let us say. Most authors just let it finish there. Some type "The End." Old newspaper veterans may type the number sign ("#######") or the number "30." I usually just conclude the story or article, and since it is obvious this is the "punch line," add nothing to it.

After you have typed your manuscript, look it over carefully. Yes, you can make neat corrections. I make them myself, rather than retype a whole page. If you have too many corrections, best put a fresh sheet into the machine and do it over.

Your manuscript is an index to you, as you present yourself and your work to the editorial eye. A sloppy manuscript indicates a writer apparently not careful. We all make mistakes, but we try to minimize them and we try not to broadcast them. The person who doesn't make mistakes doesn't exist. But when you have to correct, make it look as unobtrusive as possible. With all the new gadgets in stationery shops for typewriting erasures, this should be no problem.

And now that the piece is on the launching pad ready to zoom into the blue, where shall it land?

That's up to you. You must study the markets. Maybe you will enter it in a contest, such as the ones *Seventeen* or

Ingenue magazines run, or those put on by Scholastic Magazines, also in New York.

Maybe you will send it to a Sunday school or juvenile magazine published in Cleveland or Boston. Perhaps it is a good hobby piece and might appeal to an editor of such a periodical. Maybe it is a filler which would fit into one of the sports magazines.

Study the markets in writer's magazines like *The Writer,* published in Boston, or *The Writer's Digest,* printed in Cincinnati. These carry lists of publications and what they want by way of length and kind of story and article. From time to time they list contests held by various organizations and publishers.

The writer's magazines also contain much material to inspire and instruct budding authors (and more experienced ones, too). Writers share experiences just as I am with you.

After surveying the field, and making a decision to send your script to a particular house, secure a legal-sized envelope, 4⅛″ x 9½″, fold your script twice to fit in, fold and enclose a similar envelope, self-addressed and stamped (for the return of the manuscript if it is not accepted), address the outside envelope and send it off. Address it to: "Editor, Hobbies, Inc.," or whatever the name of the periodical may be, making sure you write the correct address on the succeeding lines. Make sure your name and address are on the back.

In my case, even before going to the mailbox, I take the carbon copy of the script and somewhere in the large three-inch space between my name and address in the upper left section and the title below, I write the name of the periodical and the date sent. I file this in my large folder, which is kept chronologically, the latest story or article on top.

An answer can reasonably be expected from two weeks

to two months, although there can be some wild, weird exceptions. I have written a piece and six days later had a check. I have also not heard from an editor for six months, or more.

Periodically I review material in the file. If there are some pieces way down at the bottom of the pile, sent out months before, I write a brief, polite query to the editor, inquiring about the disposition of the script.

Sometimes editors are ill, the editorial staff changes, the publishing house is revising its periodicals from weekly to monthly, from sixteen large pages to 32 smaller ones, or there is some other legitimate reason for the delay. Be patient.

I recall taking over a large stack of submitted manuscripts years ago when I was an editor. My heart sank as I saw them piled on desk and table. My predecessor had been ill and the work had piled up.

First, I placed all the envelopes in the proper chronological order, oldest in front, most recent at the end. I made long lines of these scripts, then started in on the huge task of whittling down the batch, either accepting or returning.

When a clerk would enter with another batch, I would feel I was on a treadmill, getting nowhere. So I'd take manuscripts home and read, read, read long into the night.

Finally, weeks later, only a handful of old scripts remained, and I would clean these up just in time for the boy to come in with another accumulation!

Editors must attend conventions and seminars, work with artists to illustrate pieces, consult superiors about changes in the format. This all takes time, too. They must also sometimes proofread material to be published, and lay out pages. So be patient with editors when the return mail does not bring a check or a letter glowing with praise.

At the end of this chapter I will list some of the places to send material, places where I know it will definitely be read and considered.

Some publishing houses do not read unsolicited material.

The larger magazines buy much from established authors who have agents. Although an agent cannot sell a poor manuscript, he does have personal contact with many editors, and stands a better chance to get his client's work read. This is not to suggest that non-established authors are not occasionally printed. But they are rare exceptions to the rule.

Most authors must work themselves up through the

"minor leagues," becoming better known, more talented, more interesting. Then they hit the big time.

Send to the markets you stand a reasonable chance of cracking, or at least, of getting an encouraging word. Don't try to compete with the experts.

The manuscript is on its way. Take care of it, Mr. Postman! Try to find a home for it, or bring it back unsmudged and as neat as when it was sent out, that another spot for it may be found as soon as possible!

Write a 300-400 word composition on one of the following or any other topic you are interested in:

"The Professional Appearance of a Manuscript"
"The Trials and Tribulations of an Editor"
"Age Is No Barrier to Success in Writing"

Any new ideas? Write them down here:

At this point let me say a few words about contests. Although you will find at the end of this chapter a list of publishing houses that receive contest material slanted for young people, other places consider manuscripts sympathetically, too. Often the American Legion, or the Veterans of Foreign Wars, or some religious or political organization sponsors a writing contest.

The World's Fair sponsored such a contest years ago before the exposition opened at Flushing Meadows. Students were awarded bonds and medals, one of the usual ways such winners are recognized. In other contests, essays on fire prevention, ways to improve communities, suggestions for public welfare are solicited.

Contests are held by newspapers for the best weekly letter submitted by a teenager. Sometimes magazines hold such contests, or request answers to problems posed by a writer or editor.

Don't shun such opportunities. They are "markets," too. Sometimes the rewards are greater than what you might receive from acceptance by a magazine. Added publicity, recognition, and expensive prizes may accompany the major award.

One of my earliest bits of writing was part of a contest run by a religious publishing house. It requested material (800 word articles) for a series of seven tracts (small booklets). Included were such subjects as "The Value of Regular Church Worship," "Stewardship of Time, Talents and Possessions," "Why You Should Study the Bible," "The Art of Prayer."

I decided to write an article on each of the seven divisions of the contest. The best tract in each division was to be published for general distribution to the churches, and the writer would win $20. (This was some years ago, when $20 seemed impressive.) I thought that by entering all seven divisions I would stand a good chance of winning at least one of the $20 prizes.

No, I didn't win—or did I? I received a letter from the publishing house advising me that although none of my tracts was judged worthy of a first prize, three of them were so good they wanted to publish them and would pay me $5 each. That was $15, almost as much as a first prize!

Don't neglect contests. Find out all you can about the competition. Make sure you qualify, for sometimes the age of the entrant is a factor. If it's for junior high students and you are in the senior high, you are not eligible. If it's for seniors only, and you are not a senior when you enter, don't try to fool anyone. You will only make trouble for yourself. Be sure you qualify.

Get all the material you can on the contest. Folders or pamphlets usually describe the competition. Digest it all thoroughly. If it's on a historical aspect of American life, do some research, "go the second mile." Don't just get a cursory idea of the salient material. Most of the other contestants will do only that. Dig out unusual material that will make your stuff sparkle.

Use your ingenuity. Don't depend on the material in your school's library, good as that may be. Make a trip to some other source for that "off-trail," out of the ordinary material. It may be the town historian, an old member of your church, an American Legionnaire, a member of the Daughters of the American Revolution, the fire department captain.

Follow the same procedure for writing essays or articles. Digest all the material. Lay it out for use on small pieces of paper or cards, and then start a first draft. Use incidents, illustrations, dialogue, if length permits. Write a corking good opening, a sizzling conclusion.

Type it as neatly as you can, retype it if necessary. Make sure you get it in before the deadline. If there are other requirements, such as a photograph of yourself, or a letter from your teacher or principal, make sure this is included. If it all has to be received in a certain sized envelope, make sure you follow instructions to the letter. Check that you have followed all the requirements before submission. Sometimes a good paper is disqualified simply because a contest rule has been violated.

Then rest back—just like after sending in a story or article to a magazine—rest just long enough to catch your breath and start work on your next piece. For that is the best remedy to avoid the impatience blues which strike while waiting word from an editor. Keep busy on research, keep going, keep gathering facts and ideas.

This is the method used by professional writers. They don't write one piece, then sit back, nervously biting their nails and waiting for results. They move on to the next subject. That's why one of them said once, "What is my best story? My next one."

While this may seem to be a side issue, let me speak for a few moments about photographs. Sometimes a listing of markets suggests that photographs are desired. You may be able to get them from a chamber of commerce or some industrial firm, or you may be able to take them yourself.

If an editor has your article and writes for pictures, make sure you identify the photos with your name and address. This can be written lightly on the back in the upper right hand corner. Don't dig into the photo.

Some writers paste a typed description of the photo with their name and address on the back. Some type the caption such as "The coach speaks to the team before each game," on a sheet which is then clipped to the photo, the clip not covering any major part of the photo. Make sure the request "Please return to ________" is also on the back.

Whether or not the editor uses the photo, he will send it back to you. You may be able to make use of it on some other occasion, or if it is a borrowed photo, you are obligated to return it.

It is surprising how often I have used my own photos,

taken with a less than $10 camera, to illustrate my pieces. I do not claim to be a great photographer, and sometimes I have been very discouraged with the results; then again, my pictures have been good enough to run in magazines with national coverage. Clarity is the keynote, good contrast of the person from his background so that heads don't merge with trees or mountains.

Sometimes dull, flat photos will reproduce, but usually the request is for "glossies."

To make sure you are turning out the sort of copy the magazine you are trying to hit will use, buy or send for a sample copy or two. When you write, say you are willing to pay the cost of a sample copy, and also enclose stamps.

Sometimes you'll receive a mimeographed sheet, listing requirements. Often the specifics are somewhat demanding. Yet these requirements are no more unreasonable than those rules listed for contests.

Study sample copies thoroughly. Do more than note the kind of stories or articles used. See what else the periodical contains. Sometimes it has advertisements, or fillers. They are a good index to what kind of publishing house and editor you are dealing with.

Some church publishers are "conservative" in approach. They like the Bible used in some way in all stories and articles. Others are not as "conservative," but deal with issues growing out of one's religious life, including school life, politics, or similar, secular areas.

Usually when a periodical is for 12, 13, and 14 year olds, the editors like the hero or heroine of a story to be a few years older. Most young people like to look ahead in their life, to what they will be. The protagonist of a 12 to 14 paper is usually a senior high student.

Study the material in the sample copy to see the type of material the editor is buying. Don't poll-parrot the same sport or activity, but remember that if he took a sports story, he (or she) may take another.

For practice a young writer may rewrite the opening of a published story or article, to see whether or not the newer version is more interesting. Sometimes his opening is actually better.

In some cases, the editor knows he has not printed the greatest story in the world, but at that time, he had to fill up his pages, and it was the best he had.

Finally, remember, most magazines and church periodicals often publish as much as five to six months ahead. That is, in April the editor looks for material for his fall issues. It is too late, usually, to send in a baseball story at Easter time though the baseball season hasn't begun.

Keep alert to this seasonal problem. I write ice hockey stories in the summer for publication in February. Sometimes an editor may receive a baseball story in July and hold it for a whole year, until the following summer, but not usually. When I was an editor, my inventory of stories and articles was about five months or so ahead.

Now I'd like to share with you some of the information I have acquired from a variety of sources, from personal meetings with editors, from writers' magazines, and from inquiries I have sent out by mail. All of the following periodicals will give your stories and articles a sympathetic hearing, and almost all of them pay for what they publish.

Action American Baptist Convention Valley Forge, PA 19481	stories and articles to 1,200 words (for teens)
Accent on Youth 201 8th Avenue, S. Nashville, TN 37203	stories and articles 1,000- 1,500 words (for teens)
Catalyst Box 179 St. Louis, MO 63166	stories and articles 1,000- 1,200 words (12-18 years)
Conquest 6401 The Paseo Kansas City, MO 64131	stories and articles to 2,500 words (teens)
Contact 44 E. Franklin Street Huntington, IN 46750	stories and articles to 1,500 words (teens)
Encounter Box 2000 Marion, IN 46952	stories and articles 1,000 words (teens)

Event 127 Ninth Avenue, N. Nashville, TN 37203	stories 1,000-3,000 words, articles 1,000-1,500 words (12-17 years)
Hicall 1445 Noonville Avenue Springfield, MO 65802	articles and stories 1,000- 1,200 words (high school)
Insight 6856 Eastern Avenue, N.W. Washington, DC 20012	1,000 word articles only (15-25)
Jet Cadet 8121 Hamilton Avenue Cincinnati, OH 45231	stories and articles to 1,000 words (9-12)
The Modern Woodmen Magazine 1701 First Avenue Rock Island, IL 61201	articles 1,500-2,000 words (11-16) (an insurance company magazine)
One 426 South Fifth Street Minneapolis, MN 55415	stories and articles 1,000- 1,200 words (upper teens)
On the Line 610 Walnut Avenue Scottdale, PA 15683	stories and articles 750- 1,000 words (10-14)
Opus One 127 Ninth Avenue, N. Nashville, TN 37203	religious music articles about 1,000 words (9-12)
Power 1825 College Avenue Wheaton, IL 60187	stories and articles to 1,000 words (older teens)

Probe 1548 Poplar Avenue Memphis, TN 38104	articles to 1,500 words (boys 12-17)
Straight 8121 Hamilton Avenue Cincinnati, OH 45231	stories and articles 1,000-1,200 words (teens)
Teens Today 6401 The Paseo Kansas City, MO 64131	stories and articles to 1,500 words (15-18)
Venture Box 150 Wheaton, IL 60187	stories and articles 1,000-1,500 words (boys 10-18)
Young Ambassador Box 82808 Lincoln, NB 68501	articles and stories to 2,000 words (early teens)

Here, then, are twenty places to write for sample copies, so that you can study the material published. Some of these publications are weeklies, some monthlies, some take mostly short stories, some like essays. Most of them take both.

Write for current information as requirements constantly change. This is a field where, even if you get a cold, printed rejection slip, you can be assured that your material was read.

Start accumulating your own file of sample copies of papers and magazines, so that you can slant your material to the right market. Read the writers' magazines to learn of new periodicals, too. Since they have no established group of writers, yet, they may be receptive to new writers.

Write a 300-400 word composition on:

"The Market for Teenage Reading"
"A Contest I'd Like to Enter"
"Research Is Important"
"Photos Help Sell an Article"
or some optional topic

Any new ideas occur to you while reading this chapter? Write them down here for development later:

Chapter 8

The Returned Manuscript

"I press toward the mark for the prize of the high calling of God in Christ Jesus" *(Philippians 3:14).*

Your well typed, well constructed story or article has been mailed. You continue getting ideas for your next story or essay. You remain busy as a creative writer, which is the mature, professional way.

Then one day the postman brings a fat envelope to your door. It's your "masterpiece," turned down unceremoniously by some inconsiderate editor who hasn't seen fit to publish it.

The dull, desolate feeling is beyond description. In a highly emotional state, you consider the whole matter. Why, I followed all the rules suggested; why wasn't it accepted? What's wrong with that editor? Doesn't he (or she) recognize good writing?

Later, when you cool off, you begin to evaluate the situation more objectively. You may come to several conclusions:

1. You're not a writer. You never were, and never will become one. You've just been "kidding" yourself. Forget the whole idea.
2. Maybe you have to know an editor personally to get printed. Why not visit one?
3. Better still, why not buy your own publishing house and print all your own stuff? In this way, you will not have to give some silly editor the opportunity to turn down your "deathless prose."

With regard to that third possibility, maybe you will

first have to marry a rich person, but that is a secondary obstacle on your way to literary success. You can take care of that item in due course.

Buying one's own publishing house, however, is not the usual way to become a successful author.

Visiting editors is also a costly scheme. In the first place, they are usually far away, and in the second, they are probably too busy to see you. After an author becomes fairly well known, editors can be contacted.

In New York on other business, I telephoned Dr. Kenneth L. Wilson, whom I knew slightly; he listened to a couple of ideas I wanted to write about. I asked him whether he thought he might like to see them if I went ahead and finished them. He referred me to another editor on the *Christian Herald* staff who on the phone discarded two of the three ideas and suggested I try the third one and send it along.

But this was an exception, and would be for the average writer, for in all the years I have been writing, the postman has been the middle man. He has brought my stories and ideas to the editor, and the editor in turn has corresponded with me, either sending a check or a rejection slip.

Getting to know editors comes after you have written for them, not before.

If you can't buy your own press, or get to know an editor personally, perhaps we must consider that first possibility: you're not a writer.

Have you been kidding yourself about writing? Are you serious about it? Did you think you would get a check for $2,500 for that first effort, or even $250?

Self-confidence is fine, but let's face the facts honestly. If it were that easy to become a published pro, everyone would be doing it.

To excel in anything we must practice and practice—and have faith in eventually becoming what we want to become. The combination of hard work and faith makes successful, even great writers.

Perhaps the first supposition is partly correct. You are not a real writer, yet. But you have faith in yourself, and you are willing to continue. That is what is important.

Recently, I read a report that 28% of the students who enter college do not return at the end of the first year. A high attrition rate, but it has been substantiated. Some of these students probably didn't have the ability, and some didn't have the stick-to-it-iveness to continue when the going became rough.

The going is rough whenever a beloved manuscript comes home, too. But when the rejections come, what you do about them is the key to your writing character. Will you be like one of the 28% in college who drop out at the first sign of defeat? Will you say: I'm not a writer, I was just kidding myself, and I guess I'll forget it?

If you do drop out of the race, then you truly are not a writer. Remember, a writer must have a tough skin, must be able to "take it."

So maybe you are right in your analysis of yourself. You are not a writer—and will never be one. Unless you resolve to knuckle down and get to work!

Now that you have resolved to carry on, analyze your article or story. (Do this with any compositions marked and given back to you, whether by a teacher or an editor.)

Content and *Technique* are the two criteria. What is said and how it is said. There may be no technical errors, but the content may be dry as dust. The ideas in the piece may be good, but there may be too many technical errors.

Analyzing work rejected by editors may not be as easy as analyzing why you received such and such a mark on a school paper. The cold rejection slip says little: "We want to thank you for submitting this script to us, but we regret that it does not fit into our schedule" (or "meet our requirements"). That's all.

Why do *you* think your manuscript came back?

First, ask, was it the right length for that periodical? If you send out 2,500 word stories to places that run only 1,200 or 1,500 word stories, you have no one to blame but yourself when they bounce.

Second, was it a girl's story sent to a boy's periodical? Or an adult-told tale sent to a juvenile weekly? Remember, youth magazines don't want older folks as the heroes and heroines. Did you send it to the wrong publisher?

Third, now that you look at it, while it is well typed and neat, is it really a good story or an interesting article? Could the opening not have been a bit more dramatic? And that title, "Mulberry Blues." Just what would that have meant to an editor?

Perhaps something is wrong with it, something you could fix up. If nothing seems wrong as you scrutinize it now, fresh from the editorial desk, send it out to another editor. If it does need rethinking, now is the time to start to work.

For some writers, one of the most disagreeable tasks in the world is to renovate a script. When they first finish it, they are aglow. When asked to rewrite it, they sag. They just can't bear to cut away any of their precious, inspired verbiage.

The truth of the matter is that, in most cases, writing is improved by rewriting. No matter how dear some of those original phrases might be to you, they may have to go! And in their going, the manuscript may become ten times better.

Rewriting is a necessary evil for all writers. The sooner you learn that it is part of the writing game and dive right into it, the better.

Years ago, one of my first experiences in rewriting was on a 2,500 word short story. The editor sent it back with a brief note, "If you can cut it down to 1,500, I may be able to use it."

When I received this note, I wondered whether or not I should rewrite. I wanted to send it out as it was to another publication, thinking it might catch on there. Then I reconsidered.

All right, I'd rewrite it. So I set out to remove 1,000 words.

First with a plain lead pencil, I crossed out all the unnecessary adjectives and adverbs, the modifiers. Then I went back and counted. Only 200 words chopped.

With a red pencil I took out prepositional phrases (another form of modifier). About another 200 words or so gone. I was getting a little worried. I realized I'd have to rewrite one or two of the incidents, tighten them up by merely mentioning them, not fully describing them. Finally, when I counted again, I had about 1,500 words. I sent it in again, and it was published.

I have mentioned that when I was an editor, I never sent back a rejection slip without a brief note: "Sorry, just used a baseball story," or "Too late for this season," or even the simple, solitary word, "Overstocked."

This last word means that for the time being, the editor has purchased enough material to last him for a long while, and there is no sense in sending in anything to him; he won't even read it. But the fact that he is overstocked and tells you so brightens the day. The script has been returned, but at least the editor mentioned nothing wrong with the story or article. He just didn't have room for it at the time.

That you should appreciate the notes editors may send to you with returned material cannot be stressed enough. Some writers may expect such notes, but editors are not obligated to write anyone. All they have to do is accept material or reject it. You sent it in the first place. They didn't ask you to.

When an editor sends back a note, appreciate it. From a busy life he has taken the moments to address you and your script personally, privately. Look over the note and consider whether or not it really applies to your story or article. And if it does, then a rewrite is in order.

Editors can be wrong. One editor can turn down a script and another accept it eagerly. For some time I sold scripts regularly to a certain weekly. Then a new editor arrived and took none at all, yet the scripts he rejected were accepted elsewhere. Each editor has his own reasons for accepting or rejecting.

Novelist Kenneth Roberts tells of a similar experience. He was selling regularly to a national weekly which suddenly turned down one of his manuscripts. He sent it to another, which wrote back that it was "just the thing they were looking for."

So editors can be wrong. In fact, when a script comes back, try to be philosophical, and say, "Well, that's just one man's opinion. Someone else may want it."

Many writers go to writer's conferences to have their work analyzed by editors and other authors. I have sat in sessions where plotting, characterization, background were all discussed by an expert in the field. Sometimes such meetings are fruitful beyond measure. They are worthwhile when the budding author takes to heart the well-considered evaluation and suggestions of experienced writers.

Before accepting anyone else's suggestions for improvement, many authors try to stand off from their work, try to see it from an objective viewpoint. This is not easy. I try to do it myself. Having sat on both sides of the editorial desk, I try to see it from the editor's standpoint.

I write my script. Then I type the envelope for the editor and my self-addressed, return envelope and stamp it. Then I fold the script and place it in the envelope to the editor. After a moment or two, pretending I am the editor, I take out the script.

I say to myself, I am an editor receiving this script. What is my first reaction? Is it neatly typed? Is it well titled? Does it interest me at once?

Difficult as it is to appraise one's own efforts, if one is successfully to promote his own writing, something of this kind of analysis must be done. We can't offer every script to an editor at a writer's seminar. A teacher isn't always at hand to give opinions.

Try such self-analysis on your scripts. See whether or not you can stand off from the finished product and pretend to be an editor looking it over.

Some students develop self-analysis rather easily and can look over a first draft and know instantly how to improve it.

Above all, when you receive setbacks, try to be professional. The baseball player who grounds out to end the game does feel badly. But he knows that tomorrow, another game goes on, and he can't waste time mooning over the game lost. He shrugs it off as best he can, and resolves to do a better job the next time.

When you do have to settle down and rewrite a piece, take it in your stride. Be on the alert for what may have tripped you up. Was it merely mechanics? Was it something in the structure of the plot?

In our classes I always offer everyone a chance to rewrite any composition, within a reasonable time, say a week. Thus industrious and intelligent students are rewarded for renewed effort. They realize that not only is there a chance of a better mark, but they indeed will be writing an improved paper.

Never think that your original effort is sacrosanct. Never feel that the entire piece should not be revised. I had to do that with a script which "bounced" a dozen times. After two rewrites, it finally clicked.

Maybe your piece needs a different beginning. Perhaps it should have a different ending. Maybe dialogue needs brushing up, a little more like life.

In the last half of this chapter we want to talk about the three major ways you can rewrite. But it's time now for some fingering of the "scales of the piano." A writer has to write, you know!

Write a 300-400 word composition on one of the following topics, or some optional topic:

"Scripts, Too, Have Feelings"
"The Successful Writer's Key Characteristic—Persistence"
"When Rejections Come"
"The Value of Analyzing Your Own Work"
"Rewriting—the 'Necessary Evil'"

Basically you should rewrite for one of two reasons: mechanics or effect. Either you have technical mistakes to eliminate or structure to revamp. These two thoughts, then, should be in your mind as you start to operate on your story or article.

Some writers go over a rejected piece to see whether or not mechanical mistakes should be rectified; then they scrutinize it a second time for structural errors that destroy the desired effect.

Take the time first to look for grammatical errors. Then read it over again to see whether or not more than merely incorrect use of tense, punctuation, or pronoun is involved.

Maybe your stuff is good, but the paragraphs are misplaced. Sometimes a fourth paragraph makes a better lead, an incident described toward the end of the piece fits in the beginning with greater effectiveness. Maybe two paragraphs should be eliminated entirely, since they do not appear to advance the plot or develop the theme.

Whether it is grammatical (technical) or structural "illness" which affects your script, authors use three methods to rewrite a literary effort. They are:

1. boiling it down
2. fattening it up
3. enlivening it

Often an article or story does not suffer at all when it is "boiled down." The term "boiling down" is an old newspaper phrase which literally means "condensing a story to permit it to occupy less space." This is done all the time in editorial offices for space is at a premium, whether it be a magazine or a newspaper. You simply cannot jam a 2,500 word yarn into space allowed for a 1,200 word story.

Eliminate extraneous, unnecessary words and phrases, keep the "meat" of the story or article, and the reader doesn't have to plow through useless verbiage.

The "boiling down" process, however, can be harmful, if not handled carefully.

The writing of a précis is good practice for all writers. Take a longer work and reduce it to a brief summary. You will have far less space than the original writer had to splash around in. You will have to confine your writing to, say, eight lines, when he used 35. All of this means you have to be careful just which words you do use.

Make a note of the précis as another way to learn how to write effectively. It is as valuable a practice to a budding author as setting-up exercises are to a football player. At the moment, that is all it is—practice, exercise, but it is an aid to technique.

But you are not going to make a précis out of your story or article. You simply want to trim it.

It is amazing how many words we all use which are unnecessary. They are "dead wood," they do not move a story along. Such phrases as "identically the same" or "a round circle" are good examples.

A "favorite" of some editors is "because of the fact that." "Because of the fact that Jack could not come, the date was cancelled." Five words occur in the phrase "because of the fact that," when one alone, "because," is all that is needed. "Because Jack could not come, the date was cancelled."

One of the best ways to cut is to eliminate modifiers. You may be using too many adverbs or adjectives, or both. "The squat, ugly, ill-tempered and snarling ape glared at

his keeper." What can be eliminated without disturbing the thread of the story?

What would you take out, if you had to condense? "squat, ugly, ill-tempered"? Perhaps. It all depends upon what effect you want, and how much you really have to pare the sentence.

In addition to eliminating single modifying words, you should consider prepositional phrases. These, too, act as adverbs and adjectives. Replace the prepositional phrase with a single adverb or adjective. Instead of "the book with the red cover," you might want to say "the red book."

Just as individual words and phrases can be eliminated, so can modifying clauses, those longer groups of words found in complex sentences. These adjectival and adverbial clauses offer little really vital information. The grammarians call them "nonessential clauses."

Such nonessential clauses are usually set off from the rest of a sentence by commas. Their omission does not alter the meaning of the sentence or make it nonsensical. They simply add information, information not really important.

In the complex sentence: "Harvey Johnson, who used to go to Melrose High, has moved next door to me," the adjective clause "who used to go to Melrose High" is considered nonessential. It can be eliminated and the sentence can simply read: "Harvey Johnson has moved next door to me."

Adverbial clauses cannot be eliminated so easily when one is condensing, but sometimes a single adverb can take the place of six in an adverbial clause. "As noiselessly as he possibly could, Milt opened the door." In this case we might simply want to write "Noiselessly, Milt opened the door."

You will have to guide yourself accordingly, as you chop down, for you know what you want to say and how. When you have to eliminate words, however, you have little choice but to turn clauses into phrases and phrases into single words.

In boiling down, be careful about removing entire paragraphs. This is an easy way to reduce a story or article, but may result in making your piece sound "choppy" or jerky. Don't heedlessly strike out paragraphs.

Two paragraphs might be merged into one, however, with a shortening of one or both.

Are you able to condense the thought in two or three paragraphs into one solid paragraph? This is no easy feat —the ability to do so must be developed. An entire paragraph often can be reduced to one sentence and nothing important eliminated.

Additions and deletions. These are the two words to keep in mind when revising. Additions lead us to discuss "fattening."

Although a piece can be fattened by simply reversing the procedure for boiling it down, this is not usually what creative writers and editors have in mind. If a piece is too "sketchy," the writer probably did not do enough research on it, or is repeating facts in another manner. Nothing is being done to advance plot or develop theme.

To say in one place that "500,000 citizens pay taxes in our county" is no different from "half a million pay taxes." If you repeat the facts, using a different kind of phraseology, you have not "fattened the piece." Or if you have, you have simply added some "blubber."

Professional writers sometimes claim that only ten percent of their facts, dug up by diligent research, ever show in the final published article. They feel it is far wiser to have more material than you need than to skimp on research and try to stretch a 1,000 word script to 3,500.

If asked to develop or fatten a 1,000 word script to 3,500, such authors already have the material to do so. They write about other aspects of their subject, using the facts they already have in their files.

On the other hand, if they did not do too good a job of original research, they must go back to gather more data.

You may need new facts. You may have them handy, or you may have to go to sources other than your file, depending upon your previous research.

You may have enough factual information at hand, in fact, right in your article, but you haven't thoroughly explored its value. You've skipped lightly over some phase of your topic that very well might be developed.

In this case you will be more descriptive, perhaps, or try to enlarge your reader's horizon by pointing out still another avenue of thought. "Not only should you consider this," you imply as you add to your piece, "here is something else to bear in mind."

Fattening an article simply for the sake of length is wrong. Merely adding words, phrases, or paragraphs does not enhance.

You want to give your editor more of the good material already offered; you want to say, "Here is another spoonful of this delicious concoction." And as he eats, you want him to say, "Say, that's all right! This is as delectable as the first mouthful!"

All of this leads us to the third way to improve material. We call it "enlivening," really substitution.

The words originally written didn't "click." How often have I written that on a script I returned! You may have taken a terrific cut at the ball, true, but you didn't connect.

In this case, you must overhaul the piece. Sometimes one method is more effective than another. One aspect of the piece must be brightened more than another. You have good facts. You just sounded too much like an encyclopedia.

Or perhaps your dialogue needs to sparkle more, needs some metaphors and similes.

"I couldn't talk. When I finally found my voice, all that could come out was 'what, what, what, what?'

"'Stop sputtering like a run-down engine!' Bud commanded."

Maybe you need a new lead. The one you now have doesn't reach out and "hook" the reader.

Perhaps you need a different ending. The end doesn't satisfy in its present form. It isn't quite the right "tag line."

Perhaps you will have to shift emphasis. An article about radio, TV, and other personalities who visit our veterans' hospitals to record programs by the servicemen, could be handled several ways. First it might be written from the standpoint of the people who go in and place the microphone at the bedside for the veterans to speak into. You might emphasize that people from the entertainment world are truly doing a wonderful social service. They are to be commended for giving their time. This is a labor of love, they are forgetting themselves to remember others.

You might want to switch emphasis to tell the story from the viewpoint of the nurses, doctors, and administrators. "You don't know how much you've helped us in our work with these soldiers, sailors, marines, and airmen!"

Or, your emphasis might be on the men themselves. "It makes me feel like I'm really somebody when you folks come in and let me enact a role in an old radio skit," a grateful veteran says to a TV actress.

Similarly, you may have written a short story from the wrong viewpoint. Maybe you wrote it in third person when you should have written it in the first person, and not from the hero's viewpoint but from that of his buddy or pal. You can sometimes make your tale more effective if, like Arthur Conan Doyle, you use a "Dr. Watson" occasionally to tell your reader what a "great guy" your hero really is.

Shifting from third to first person often "makes" a short story. In an article, shifting from either a first or third to a "you-are-there" second person viewpoint is often best.

Far too often writers do not get readers involved in their problem or topic. If the article is one in which the author wants them to do something, the use of the second person is valuable. "Your money is going down the drain," or "You may yourself some day have to face this situation."

Sometimes in a short story, you might have too many characters, confusing the reader, not allowing each character to contribute his full share to the development of the plot. You might tighten your story and make it more convincing by eliminating one or two.

Just as you might have too many persons in your story, so you might have too many scenes. A story is like a motion picture or TV show unrolling before the eyes of your reader. You can't have your hero or heroine jumping from spot to spot, like a flea on a hot frying pan.

Your yarn or article may need a different title, although often a good story or article is taken by an editor who changes the original title himself.

But there is a reason for mentioning a new title. If you start thinking about a new title, you might also start thinking about a whole new emphasis, or a new plot twist. You might think of developing one character instead of another. Usually the more thinking you do about a literary project, the better it becomes.

As you review your work, ask yourself, too, whether you have appealed to all five (or as many as feasible) of the senses. Have you tried to make your reader not only see, but hear, touch, taste, and smell? Such restructuring of your script might be the solution.

You might have taken six hours to gather material and write your first script. The revision might have taken almost as long, but good writing consists of rewriting.

Always make your first effort as good as you can, but be prepared to revise it all. And don't be disappointed when your material is rejected or criticized as not having quite hit the mark. Anything worth criticizing is worth rewriting. Tomorrow is another day—when your work will be much better than yesterday's. Every composition written should be a step forward on the writing trail to a successful future as an author.

Write a 300-400 word composition on one of the following topics, or some topic that appeals to you:

"Boiling It Down"
"How to 'Fatten' a Script"
"The Value of Writing a Précis"
"Enlivening the Story (or Article)"
"The Right Viewpoint Is Important"
"Too Many Characters Spoil the Broth"

Have any new ideas for future writing occurred to you since reading this chapter or while going through it? Write them here for future writing.

Chapter 9

The Teacher-Student Consultation

"The same commit thou to faithful men, who shall be able to teach others also" *(II Timothy 2:2)*.

Each summer at scores of colleges and resorts, embryonic authors attend special writers' conferences. These are listed in the various writers' magazines earlier in the year to permit budding authors to reserve places at the lectures and seminars.*

At such writers' workshops successful authors and editors discuss writing techniques. Often the work of writers who have not yet sold material is read and analyzed, both by fellow students and the professional editor or writer in charge. In addition, each student is granted a personal conference.

*Seventy-seven such writer's workshops are listed annually in the April issue of *The Writer*.

Professional and beginner sit down and review a piece of work done by the latter. Personal conferences may teach writers as much as or more than the more formal lectures.

In fact, many writers-to-be sign up for such courses mainly to be able to sit down with a pro to learn "tricks of the trade." A suggestion here and one there may enable a new author to improve his script or encourage him to do a better job.

In school your teacher enacts the role of the "pro" writer or editor at summer workshops. When your teacher sits down with you to review your work, don't let your mind wander. Everything he or she says is important. Don't waste these precious moments of personal evaluation of *your* work.

As bromidic as it sounds, two heads are usually better than one. Your teacher has studied literature, knows the writing field. So listen, and make notes as he discusses your script.

In our Creative Writing classes I usually set one or two days a week aside for such personal conferences. After a few compositions have been written, we begin scheduling students. Then, while most students are writing or rewriting a paper, I sit down with an individual student and together we go over his papers.

If we are looking over a short story, plotting may be a weakness, or dialogue, or characterization. We discuss it, make suggestions, and ask where improvement could be made. Now that he is looking at his work from a distance, the student often sees what he has written differently.

Personal evaluation of one's writing by a more experienced person is of great value. When I went to high school, we had no such personal criticism by teachers. In fact, we did not even have Creative Writing classes. Later I paid for special criticism, took writing courses, both in college and by correspondence, purchased books to learn more about writing, and attended summer workshops.

When a teacher discusses your writing, you can adopt one of three attitudes:

1. Agree when he suggests changes.
2. Disagree.
3. Be indifferent.

Sometimes, not often, a student appears indifferent; he seems to feel that he knows what he wants to write and how he wants to write it, that the instructor is not conversant with what he is trying to get across, his goals.

In such cases the iron curtain descends, the flaps of the

student's ears come down, shutting out anything the teacher is saying. The glazed look comes into the eye, and the teacher knows very well that the student has turned off his reception.

Be alert, take it all in, concentrate on what is being told you. In years to come early advice may mean money, fame, fortune, success in the writing field.

It may be a mere phrase or two—"Watch those fragments!"—or something longer, a whole paragraph of suggestions. Note them, hear them, write them down. The human memory is a faulty device. Advice written down you will always have.

Even if you may not get much actual technical help, a writing instructor can encourage. The very fact that someone is discussing your writing future sparks you. Probably this is one reason writers go to summer seminars and workshops. They need the encouragement of knowing others are interested.

You may disagree with a teacher, editor, or writer who has sat down with you to discuss your work. That's your second alternative. Nothing is wrong with that at all.

In fact, sometimes when we disagree with people, we do our best work! Friendly pats on the back are all right, but they usually do not change a fault.

When I read a short play of mine to a friend, he laughed his head off. Later I realized he did not laugh because the play really tickled him, but because he was my friend and wanted to please me.

A person unconcerned with friendship may be in a better position to disagree, point out mistakes, suggest where you went off the track. Such criticism may be justified or it may not. Teachers sometimes make mistakes!

You may be right to disagree with the criticism offered you. In fact, you might become good and angry, "blow your stack." "What kind of a suggestion is that?" you might ask, not feeling the criticism is valid.

If you get excited about criticism, that is certainly much better than being indifferent. If you are excited about something, you usually do something about it. It might not always be the right step to take, but at least you aren't being passive.

Sometimes vehement disagreement with a critic is just what you need to get going in the writing field. Years ago I wrote a radio script about the birth of Jesus Christ that was turned down. I felt it was worthy of air-time and I was determined to place it. And I did, on another station. Later, it was published in a book of radio plays.

To disagree is your prerogative, but don't be disagreeable. Be gracious. Discuss the matter as much as you can with your instructor. You want to learn, and after all, no one is infallible.

Frank McCormick was a tall, husky youth who wanted to become a major league first baseman. One afternoon the New York Giants had a tryout session for prospective players. McCormick showed up.

Manager Bill Terry speculated about the boy's possibilities, then called him over. Terry himself had been one of the game's greatest first sackers.

"Listen, kid," he told McCormick. "You're wasting your time. You'll never make it to the big leagues, so stop kidding yourself."

McCormick was discouraged, but only temporarily. He disagreed with the Giant manager. He felt he was big league timber, and he determined to prove it.

After a tryout with the Cincinnati Reds, he was sent to a farm team, and before he knew it, was playing at Crosley Field in Ohio. He became an integral part of the Reds' infield, helped them win pennants in 1939 and 1940, the World's Championship the latter year. And in 1940 the Bronx player who was told by Terry he was not of major league calibre was voted the Most Valuable Player in the National League!

People who judge you and your work *do* make mistakes. You *do* have a chance to disagree with them. When you do, maybe you will go out and show them up. Maybe you don't agree with what I am saying in this book. Show me I'm wrong. And write and tell me about it! More power to you! But write! That's my message.

By and large, you will probably agree with most of your instructor-evaluator's comments. Since he or she is older, more experienced, and more detached from your manuscript, his or her judgment is usually valid and certainly useful.

Wasted verbiage may be pointed out. "This whole paragraph is unnecessary in view of what you have just written (or what you say later), so let's eliminate it, or cut it down."

Changing certain words for better emphasis and effect may be suggested. Young writers tend to use pedantic phraseology to show off a prodigious vocabulary. A newspaper cartoon illustrates my point.

A cub reporter was being "blasted" by his editor. "Isn't 'howl' a good enough word for you? Well, if it is, then don't use 'ululate'!"

So you see, we are back to an earlier chapter on "Words," the keystone to writing success, the tools with which you fashion your "edifice," your story or article.

Your teacher may suggest, also, that you are using too many trite expressions. Are you?

Since our language is filled with clichés, all of us are prone to use them. We find them printed time and time again and wonder how they got by. They slip into all kinds of writing, daily and school newspapers, magazine stories and articles, books, reports, letters.

Once such phrases seemed sparkling metaphors and similes, lifting writing above the commonplace. But repeated usage dulled their glitter. They are more than a bore, they retard thinking.

You can have fun playing with bromides, clichés, trite expressions. Today everything from a dead body, an apple from a tree, a book from a desk, lands "with a dull, sickening thud!" You can take some of these "gems" and write a whole story using them, but your work will sound like a 1900 melodrama.

For practice, it might be worthwhile to take a dozen or so of these once shining expressions and rewrite them. What could you do with such phrases as:

"the hand that rocked the cradle"
"worked like a Trojan"
"specimen of humanity"

"sadder but wiser"
"method in his madness"
"all is not gold that glitters"
"never in the history of"
"hungry as bears"
"doomed to disappointment"
"wended their way"
"last but not least"
"as luck would have it"
"all work and no play"

Add some more of your own, collected from your own reading and listening. Even your own writing?

Avoid the cliché—like informal English you can get away with it in conversation but not in writing.

Many teachers require students to keep a "log" or error chart, checking off technical mistakes, such as punctuation errors, run-on sentences, fragments, incorrect use of pronoun, shift in tense, or misspelled words. It is assumed that such technical matters have been noted by the student before he sits down with the teacher for evaluation.

Your teacher may ask you to read aloud some of your dialogue, asking, "Does it really sound authentic?"

It is surprising how artificial dialogue may sound when read aloud. Sometimes it "kills" the character you are letting talk; he does not come across. If he is not a well-educated character and sounds like an Oxford professor, he becomes unreal.

Sometimes the plot of a story is not well constructed. Your teacher may suggest that you revise. This does not always mean discard the whole story. In fact, it is wise to keep all your efforts. Professional authors often keep scripts from which, perhaps much later, they may take a character, a scene, or a background and utilize it in a new story.

Keep your scripts to see how you are advancing in writing more effectively. It is highly stimulating to compare a story you wrote years before with your latest effort.

"Did I really write that way?" you ask yourself. "How could I!"

Your teacher may suggest that you have shifted your viewpoint. First you told the story from the main character's viewpoint, then changed to a minor character's. Or you shifted from the omniscient to the secondary character's limited vision.

Your teacher may recommend that you stop trying to make punctuation marks do the work normally assigned to words. A poorly written sentence with an exclamation point after it is a poor substitute for a truly exclamatory statement. Some young writers throw these punctuation marks around with abandon, thinking it makes for dramatic writing.

Think about every suggestion made. If you are to rewrite the piece within a certain period, make sure you have all the notes necessary. Look over your notes when the conference is over, making sure that they are legible.

Incorporate all of the suggestions made, rewrite with as much care as you can, and you will very probably see a much improved story or article.

Write a 300-400 word composition on one of the following, or some optional topic:

"Beware of the Bromide"
"The Value of Teacher-Student Conferences"
"Clichés I Can't Stand"
"Persistence"
"The Player Who 'Failed'"
"Disagreement Doesn't Mean Inaction"
"Summer Conferences"
"Keep Those Old Scripts"

Teacher-student conferences are scheduled regularly in many high school English classes, but your teachers may not follow this valuable procedure. What can you substitute?

If you are truly serious about developing writing skills, you might request an English teacher to review your work. I constantly meet students who have come to know me somehow, even though they have never been in my English, Journalism, or Creative Writing classes. I am flattered that they ask me to review material.

Sometimes a student interested in writing but unable to take Creative Writing in high school may find help and inspiration in a book on Creative Writing.

Although we have warned about letting friends see your work, short of conferences and books, you may have to resort to a friend. You might ask a retired teacher or even a relative who knows something about the field of English.

To be successful, should a writer have a literary "agent," that middle-man, who stands between author and editor?

"Agents" are of every kind. In some writer's magazines,

they advertise their services. Study this field a bit before leaping into it and sending them a script, together with a "reading fee."

Professional literary agents usually deal only with selling authors, not embryonic writers. They take the work of professional writers and "peddle" it. Such a literary agent is not a teacher.

He wants a finished job, a professional effort, to look over before sending it to an editor. He expects the writer in his "stable" to be a "pro" who knows how to write and who will produce enough salable copy each year to make handling him worthwhile.

The agent gets 10% of each sale. If he sells a story for $1,000, he gets $100, forwarding the remaining $900 to the author. If he gets $750 for an article, he takes his $75 and forwards the remainder to his client.

Out of his percentage the agent has to maintain an office (usually in New York), a clerical staff, and pay traveling (and entertaining) costs. He has little time to act as an instructor.

A literary agent will go so far as to send back a script to a professional writer with the remark that it doesn't quite seem to be of market value, or he may even make a few suggestions by way of general overhauling, but he will not take time to analyze and criticize. An agent, after all, has a product to sell—the completed script of a writer who knows what he is writing about.

Some young writers may feel that an agent can sell a poor script because he has an "in." This is far from the truth. Many agents have established easy communication with various editors but neither the editor nor the agent can afford to push scripts unacceptable to the current market.

Suppose an agent offers an inferior manuscript to an editor. The latter may look at it, and finding it inferior, lose respect for the agent's judgment.

On the other side of the editorial desk, suppose an editor personally knows and likes an agent who hands him a script that is not up to the editor's magazine standards. If the editor takes it just to do the agent a favor, the editor may soon hear about it. His reputation may suffer, and he will blame the agent and drop him.

What then are the duties of a literary agent?

The literary agent handles most of the marketing and related business with which a professional writer does not want to be bothered. He submits scripts to the places he thinks best.

He studies the markets, and knows them well. He has his finger on the pulse of editors, and often saves the time of an author who might be sending material to the wrong places.

He deals with publishers on author's rights, relieves the creative writer of worrisome business concerns.

He is something like a sub-editor who screens out material that the editor should not bother with. For his services, he receives nothing but the 10% of each sale.

Some writers never bother with agents. They market their own material and handle their own business affairs. In fact, most writers do this in the beginning. When they have become definitely established on a professional level as a selling author, they usually turn over the business side of writing to the middle man, the agent.

Besides reputable agents, there are other people who are more teachers than agents, although some of their writers' magazine ads claim they are agents. These "representatives" will handle, review and criticize any script mailed to them—for a "reading fee."

They are teachers or instructors, but they do not always operate ethically. They will read your script and write you a note about it, but some of the claims made in the ads are dubious, such as claims to get published the work of amateur writers.

Many of these teacher-agents are reputable, however, and do give you something for your money. They may point out errors, make suggestions, and, if a script is good enough, recommend a market.

But be careful about paying out your money to such reading agents.

Writers interested in developing their talent seek help from "teachers" everywhere. Even some rejection slips give advice. One we know of has a paragraph on the back which asks,

> Have you stated the purpose of your manuscript in a paragraph, or better, a sentence, before beginning to write? If you are writing fiction, have you set up a story problem and then developed plot and characterizations to show that character, and not chance, solves the problem?

Another rejection slip has a list which includes such reasons as "Overstocked," or "Manuscript too long," "Not our type of material." The editor or editorial reader checks off one or two before returning the script.

If there is absolutely no older person, or one more experienced to whom he can turn for advice and suggestions, the young writer may have to try to evaluate material himself by comparing it with written stories and articles, or file it for future analysis. Some writers find that putting away material, then reading it in the cold, clear light of a later day, enables them to analyze better.

Above all, be flexible enough to make changes suggested, either by someone else or by your more critical self. Don't be afraid to make alterations that might make a manuscript salable. Good writing often consists of rewriting.

Write a 300-400 word composition on one of the following topics, or any optional topic:

"The Value of an Agent"
"Rejection Slips That Talk"
"The Creative Writer"
"Reading Makes a Writer"

Have any ideas for future writing occurred to you while reading this chapter? Write them on the lines below:

Chapter 10

Some Final, Practical Suggestions

"Let us hear the conclusion of the whole matter: Fear God, and keep his commandments: for this is the whole duty of man" *(Ecclesiastes 12:13).*

This is our final chapter, and I want to reiterate some of the suggestions made earlier and add a few more before I write "Finis."

First of all, I want to stress reading to become a good writer. In a recent interview, Katherine Ann Porter, author of *Ship of Fools* advises that in conducting college classes in writing she had first had to teach her students to read before she could instruct them in writing.

The real writer is an avid reader. He gains much from seeing what others have written. He finds in the Bible the genius of the writers who were inspired of God, and in

other books he finds men inspired by earthly things. He values the well-turned, gracious, almost poetic phrases of the King James version of the Bible and the modern, tight, clipped phrases of many of today's authors.

He reads biography, essay, fiction, news, and poetry. He learns from all he reads. He appreciates and is challenged by what he discovers. He even learns something from the poorer writers—how *not* to write.

Along with reading, the real writer pursues the art of research. He learns how to put his hands on information he must have to complete an article or to sketch convincingly the background of a story. Research books are old friends, he knows his way around libraries.

At home the successful writer has a few books he uses regularly. These include a good dictionary, perhaps the *World Almanac* and *Information Please Almanac,* a good Bible, a thesaurus, and perhaps a good one-volume encyclopedia. He constantly tries to verify information, and he turns regularly to these books, old, familiar companions.

He reads the writers' magazines to see what editors and other writers have to say about the writing field today. He knows it is necessary not only to keep up with marketing demands, but to develop writing skills by reading articles written by those in the field longer than he has been.

As he reads, he looks always for new ideas. He is a writer primarily, not a reader. He is one who desires to make his literary contribution. He takes notes, is alert to fleeting thoughts.

The real writer looks for encouragement, and young ones often join or form writing clubs. Students who do not have room in their schedule for Creative Writing as a class, might be invited to join.

Many professional writers belong to such clubs, which are non-profit, social or professional groups. Many of them are listed in the writers' magazines, or in *The Writer's Market,* published by *The Writer's Digest,* in Cincinnati, or *The Writer's Handbook,* published by The Writer, Inc., in Boston, Massachusetts. Some writers' clubs meet every other month to evaluate the work of new authors. Writers like to get together.

If you start such a writers' club in your school, it might meet after school, with an advisor helping to organize it. During meetings, scripts might be read and evaluated, suggestions made by members on marketing, or publication in the school newspaper. Students in Creative Writing class can contribute to non-members of the class.

At such club meetings you might invite a local reporter or feature article writer, or even a local novelist to talk or to conduct a question-and-answer session. It is not difficult to bring in such guests. One might be a teacher interested in writing, perhaps a professor from a nearby college. A public relations man from a local industrial concern might be willing to come.

Such a club can do much to keep you, yourself, going as a writer. Nothing is easier than to throw down the pen and say "What's the use?" But if you meet regularly, join with others who want to learn to write, you will find you'll help each other to go on writing.

In addition, a writers' club might be able to keep its members informed of contests for student writers. More experienced members of the club can share their knowledge with newer writers.

A writers' club may want to publish its own magazine, which could be printed or mimeographed. Although printing is expensive, some clubs have been able to sell ads and subscriptions for a small magazine, enough even to make a profitable venture.

The publication of stories, poems, and articles in such a periodical may not make anyone famous, but it will encourage a young writer, lift him up, and show him the power of the printed word. Such a magazine can lead to greater things, as when some young graduate shows a prospective employer what kind of talents he has.

The publication of a writers' club magazine will also teach a young writer something of the economics of publishing. It is a costly procedure to publish, whatever kind of printing method you use—offset, mimeograph or cold type. This knowledge can be important to any writer's background.

If a writer's club magazine is not possible, the school paper may have space for a Writers' Club Column.

All in all, a writers' club can inspire writers-to-be.

One of the most encouraging experiences of a writer's life, regardless of age, is to see his material in print. Nothing so brightens the eye and snaps the shoulders back as to see one's "masterpiece" with a by-line. Whether or not the writer is paid, the mere reproduction of his piece acts as a tonic.

Do all you can to get published, in a school paper, a local weekly, in a writers' club magazine, anywhere.

Sometimes the door to publication lies in the direction of collaboration. You and a friend might want to cooperate in a column, a story, an article. Professional collaborations are common. Recently I read of a free lance writer who was employed by our government in a foreign country. He mailed back all kinds of background material to a fellow-writer who prepared the material for publication.

All are collaborators when you write the class short story, a project mentioned earlier. Each member of the class contributes a paragraph or two until the yarn is finished.

When you think of publishing, think of all the kinds of writing. Although we have concentrated on the short story and the article, two popular forms of literary expression today, don't forget the book review, the news item, the column, the editorial needed for school newspapers.

Some students have a flair for writing dialogue and might try to write one-act plays. This is a field demanding a book of its own, but the technique can be learned. Perhaps your effort and talent should be in play writing.

The writing field today embraces TV and radio, public relations and governmental work. It is wider than ever. Communication is really writing, even if the spoken word is used, for many commentators read from prepared scripts.

In the business field, the person who can compose an effective sales letter, write a radio or TV "commercial," or prepare brochures can secure a good position, for not everyone can write with clarity, force, and conviction.

Far too often, students feel that the only outlet for truly creative writing is in a magazine or newspaper, where short stories and articles are published. There are many other avenues for the creative writer who can find a place for himself in governmental, political, or religious circles.

As one who was employed for years in the business world, I know how a superior appreciates a suggestion for a monthly sales letter, a new slogan, or some other facet of the selling game. Advertising agencies seek the creative writer to write material for all media.

Many companies publish what are called "house organs," magazines or newspapers that feature activities of the company's employees, perhaps around the world. Many of the students in our Journalism and Creative Writ-

ing classes have brought such house organs to class, and we have been amazed at the amount of writing contained in a single issue.

Some house organs are weekly four-page papers, but others are slick paper, 200-page magazines, with colored pictures and maps rivaling *National Geographic.* Many contain the same feature article writing that Sunday magazine sections of newspapers carry. Several are published in various languages. One of our students brought in a German language companion to the English copy.

Some house organs have their own staffs. Others, like *The Ford Times,* pay good money for articles from free lance writers.

The writing you turn out in your high school days may be the basis for future employment on a company periodical. Some of the experiences you are now enjoying as a student may be of great value when you enter the business world, particularly if you have written about them and so made them a crystal clear part of your life, for memory, as we have said, is not too dependable.

Another field of a slightly different background is that of technical writing. Many engineers, scientists, physicians, and industrial consultants have the knowledge, the technical "know-how," but are unable to write so that others grasp it. Technical manuals, booklets, brochures, pamphlets, and articles must be prepared for publication, but these specialists cannot handle the writing job.

Here is the place for those with knowledge of that particular field who know how to form correct and understandable sentences. This is the field for the "technical writer." While there is not too much space for his imagination to work in, the technical writer can "dramatize" to a certain extent mechanical or scientific information.

Often the brochure must be written so that the ordinary layman can understand it, and this is the place for the real writer, who can take a highly complex matter and break it down, by means of examples, illustrations, and comparisons, for the man in the street.

The need for technical writers is so great that one of the largest companies in America, General Electric, constantly seeks them. In fact, at one time such writers were so scarce, engineers were hired and taught writing.

Writers for medical journals are often not doctors but people who have studied the field, know it well, and have a facility for the written word. Some of these specialized writers draw top rates when writing not only for medical periodicals but for general publication.

We have discussed the religious field, or at least the juvenile periodical field dominated by the Sunday School publishers. All the major faiths publish a score or more weeklies, monthlies, and quarterlies, offering the free lance an opportunity to make a sale and a start in his writing career.

Many denominational publishing houses have openings for first readers (people who read the scripts which come in unheralded, and are put on the "slush pile"), as well as for sub-editors, editors, proofreaders, and advertising copywriters.

The longer one speaks of the writing field and its allied area, the more he realizes that the written word today is an essential part of our daily existence. From the flyer which comes to your home announcing the opening of a new store to the most dramatic TV show, writers are involved. Someone had to place words on a sheet of paper to convey a message.

Young people interested in acting try for summer jobs with stock companies. Here they learn the tricks of the theatrical trade. They have not been paid much, but when summer is over, they have matured and learned much about the theatre.

If you are interested in writing, you might get some sort of writing job to aid you in your development. It might be on a local newspaper, part-time, or working for a Scout troop, or for a hospital or other similar organization.

The main thing is to write, to get as much experience in some area of the writing game as possible. You will learn from sitting beside professionals in the field. You will be absorbing background material perhaps for your own stories and articles, and you will be maturing as an individual, so that your writing will reflect the thinking of a professional writer.

We have mentioned plays. Perhaps you might get a job with a local little theater. We have one in our area, which produces just one show each summer. Members are high school students, but their show is of professional calibre. And their publicity is, too, from newspaper articles to posters in store windows.

And don't forget, everything a writer experiences is grist for his literary mill. Disappointment can be turned into something valuable.

In my early writing days, I had written an article for a magazine editor who said that if I could get "forty pictures of various aspects" of a particular part of the country I had described in my article, he would seriously consider the article. I got the pictures, somehow, and they were all good, glossy shots. The editor sent the whole package back with a plain rejection slip.

I was temporarily crushed. But I rallied, rewrote the article, and sent it out with a few pictures. It was accepted by a new magazine. Then I selected a few more pictures and wrote another article, and still another. I believe I wrote at least four or five articles from the material and photos obtained for the rejected article. By the time I was through, I had made at least three times more money than I would have received from the rejecting magazine.

Disappointments can be turned into triumphs (Romans 8:28). Keep going with your writing.

Write a composition of 300-400 words on one of the following topics, or on some topic that appeals to you:

"Reading Makes the Writer"
"The Writer's Research Technique"
"A Writers' Club"
"The Writers' Club Magazine"
"I Think I'll Write a Play"
"Communication in Today's World"
"If a Typewriter Could Talk"
"The Technical Writer"

As we approach the close of this "discussion" about writing, let's talk about the "Three P's of Authorship."

The first "P" stands for Practice. There is no substitute for writing. Reading, listening, sharing ideas with others is enlightening, but the absolute necessity for a writer is to do just that—write. Pleasures have to be sacrificed. If he is to write his allotted wordage for that week, he cannot decide to look at television, play a game, go on a date.

He must arrange his time and life so that he writes regularly, not now and then. He must set goals for himself, so many words this day or week, so much to be done by a certain time. The free lance writer is free from punching a time clock for a factory or office boss, but he must account to himself for time spent. He must be his own stern boss.

This is not to say that writing cannot be fun. Shirley Jackson, who has written some unusual books, including *The Haunting of Hill House,* and the famous short story, "The Lottery," once said that for her, writing was the greatest fun in the world. She thoroughly enjoyed every minute of it.

Some writers find their assignments (given by an editor, a superior, or by themselves) to be hard work, but most enjoy writing. If they didn't, in spite of what some say, they would give it all up and get a job in a supermarket.

Whatever time you allot, try your best to keep to it. Practice and practice. Write and then write some more. And then write some more. Maybe much of it will never see the light of day. Nevertheless, keep at it. Tell yourself that each page is one step nearer success as a real writer.

Practice what this book suggests. Try writing those paragraphs mentioned in Chapter Four. Try writing a précis. Try writing or rewriting news items. Write about your friends in school, the places you visit. Write editorials and short stories or character sketches of imaginary people. Keep at it. Facility with the written word will come.

Practice in anything, if done right and regularly, leads to proficiency. Athletes find it imperative. Musicians must sit at the keyboard or wield their bow day after day. Writers must keep at it, too.

The second "P," closely related to the first, is for Perseverance.

We have spoken of those who drop out of college. They do not persevere. They do not stay with it. They are the "also-rans." They did not come out winners, for various reasons. "Demas hath forsaken me," Paul said (II Tim. 4:10).

The main reason for failure was giving up. They didn't finish the game. They threw in the towel.

To throw in the towel is all too easy. When rejections come, when no one pats you on the back, when it all doesn't seem worthwhile, you may want to give up. That is the time to keep on writing. Just keep on keeping on.

Someone once asked an athletic coach the secret of becoming a champion, and he replied, "The ability to hold on five minutes longer." Think it over.

To develop perseverance, you may have to play tricks with yourself, as suggested earlier. Everyone needs devices to help him keep on.

Sometimes the announcement to someone else that we are going to accomplish so much writing is a good device.

Sometimes someone's dare is the key.

Sometimes you have to paste up on a wall the challenge to yourself.

Perseverance in any field is the keynote.

Showman and self-made millionaire Billy Rose won the world's shorthand writing contest years ago. Having practiced until he felt confident of winning, he went ice-skating the day before the big contest. He fell and sprained his thumb. He was unable to hold his pencil properly, but he was determined. That night he tried putting a pencil in a potato, and found he could grip the vegetable with his uninjured fingers and write his shorthand. The next day, potato and all, he won the shorthand championship!

Bel Kaufman, author of *Up the Down Staircase,* popular novel about a New York City schoolteacher's first year of teaching, sold the movie rights to her book for a reputed $400,000. Her advice for students: "Tell them to sit down and write. Then read what they've written. Then tear it up! Then sit down and write some more. Then read it and tear it up!"

The third "P" stands for Polish, the rewriting necessary to succeed as a writer.

Some well known writers enjoy this phase of literary creation.

The late P.G. Wodehouse, creator of the inimitable Jeeves and Bertie Wooster, and scores of short stories and novels, said it was one of the aspects he liked best about writing.

"The hardest part for me is the actual writing of my first draft," said the English author who has been writing for the past sixty years. "Once the words are down, black on white, I find I can then easily and enjoyably see where I have to prune, alter, or add new paragraphs."

What Wodehouse said is true. The most difficult is to get down that first draft in visible form. Once it actually can be seen, and not only in the mind of the author, it is comparably easy to revise it.

Almost always the first draft needs revision. Some authors write their opening paragraphs as many as twelve times. If professional writers feel they must do this, why shouldn't younger, more inexperienced, authors-to-be?

When you are ready to polish your material, make sure it has been allowed to "cool off." If you revise right after writing, you may not be as objective as you would be later on. Let it stand for awhile.

At a later time, as you reread what you have written, try to put yourself in the reader's place. Pretend you didn't write it. Make believe you are an editor, or an editorial assistant, or just an ordinary reader of a magazine or newspaper.

Try to determine whether or not you would continue reading it for its own sake. Be as objective as you possibly can.

At some point, does the story or article seem to lag? Is there too much description retarding progress?

If there is dialogue, read it aloud. Does it sound natural? Are the characters too wordy? Would a real person talk like that?

Is the ending effective? Does it ring a bell, satisfy you as a reader, or is it a letdown?

Perhaps after you have made some changes and read it once again, you are convinced it is the best you can do. Read it again, not for style or effect, but to catch any technical errors. Punctuation all right? Spelling? Meaning? If there is doubt about any word or phrase, always look it up. Your dictionary should be at hand always.

Polish your manuscript until it is the very best you can make it. Remember: when sent off, it represents you. It is your agent.

And once again, remember that you might be asked, in spite of all you have done, to revise a script some more. Do so. It might be the last, magic touch that opens the door to publication. It might be the beginning of a valuable relationship with an editor.

O. Henry, master of the surprise ending, was one of America's greatest short story writers. Yet those who claim to know say that it was his editor who polished up the yarns, made them the classics they are. Who knows how many great authors were made by an unknown editor's work.

As a rule, you alone have to do the polishing.

In the editorial rooms of a metropolitan newspaper some time ago, waiting to see the head sports editor, I observed a writer who was typing rapidly. Finally, he pulled the sheet out of the machine, placed it in front of him, and began to use his pencil almost viciously. By revising, by polishing, he was going to get his story past the editor's desk. And on his polishing operation he spent as much time as, if not more than, he did on the original story.

Learn the art of polishing. All of which means that if you are to be your own editor, you must develop perfection in grammar, punctuation, spelling, and usage. You will have to become a master of communication.

If the three "R's" of education are basic, so are these three "P's" of writing. Make them part of your writing life. Practice, persevere, polish. You will find the effort pays off. They are a sure-fire success formula.

And be patient.

The professional baseball players call it "hanging in there."

When the Cincinnati Reds were playing a game in which they were down, 2-0, the first two men in the ninth went down, and the next man, with two strikes on him, finally walked. The next two men singled. A new pitcher was brought in for the opposing team. He walked a man. Another man singled. Suddenly, the game was tied 2-2. The Reds went on to win it with a three-run rally in the tenth inning, 5-2.

In a game the New York Yankees were playing, they were down 4-0 in the eighth inning, with two men on and two men out. Clete Boyer fouled off six pitches before lacing a double that put the Yanks back in the game. They went on to grab the game in the ninth when they scored three more times.

So "hang in there," and be patient.

It's natural to be discouraged. We're all discouraged

from time to time, but a new day always dawns. Twenty-four hours later you may have a new outlook on life. Rejected manuscripts have a way of turning into accepted ones. You may sell that piece in which you believe on the twentieth try.

Try both to challenge and encourage yourself. A writer needs both. If he isn't challenged, he doesn't exert all his energy and effort. And writing calls for encouragement; he needs "jacking up" occasionally.

When Charles Dickens' classic *Pickwick Papers* was

published, a critic of a leading London newspaper remarked:

> Mr. C. Dickens, a new author, has challenged fate with a sort of facetious miscellany compendiously titled, 'The Pickwick Papers.' We do not expect to hear more of Mr. Dickens, but we sincerely wish him a modest success in those less literary fields for which his talents seem to us best fitted.

Further, when you really have done the best you can, don't sit down and applaud yourself. Get to work on the next piece. Don't put "all your eggs in one basket."

Incredible as it may sound, an author who writes for religious publication has said that he manages to keep at least one hundred scripts out at all times!

Even as I write the last pages of this book, I have a folder filled with ideas which I am pursuing and on which I am doing research for future pieces.

In the introduction to this handbook, I stated that I was writing to offer you inspiration, information, and instruction. I hope I have done that.

Most writers maintain some sort of notebook. To encourage you to keep such a book, I suggested topics at the end of each chapter. If you have faithfully jotted down new, original ideas, this, then, may be your own, first writer's notebook. This book may truly be the storehouse from which you will draw ideas for stories and articles in years to come.

May God bless you as you write, and may your literary creations see the light of publication!

Has anything occurred to you while reading these last pages? Why not jot down those ideas right here for future development.

Index

BIBLE REFERENCES

ABOUT THE BOOK

Getting published is the practical theme of this text-handbook for new writers. Unlike other writing texts which deal only with nitty-gritty grammar and dull rhetoric, this book views writing as an everyday apprenticeship, not as a classroom exercise. It is designed to be used either in high school writing classes, particularly in Christian day schools, or by individuals.

The book intersperses practical suggestions with anecdotes and personal examples to encourage budding authors to write and keep writing, to submit and re-submit articles or short fiction for publication. The ten chapters treat such topics as word awareness, vocabulary development, finding and developing ideas, rewriting, manuscript format. It includes specific information on marketing, writers' clubs and conferences, agents, industrial house organs. A market guide to magazines that publish free-lance materials is included, with addresses, types of materials, and age of readership.

The book contains so many helpful hints that the reader-writer will want to keep it as a handy guide for future reference. Space is provided for jotting down ideas and notes, making the text the apprentice-writer's note-book.

This book was designed by Publishers Graphics.
The text has been set in 12/14 Baskerville, justified.
Chapter titles are in Futura Light.
Illustrations and jacket are by Ed Parker.

ABOUT THE AUTHOR

William Folprecht is an accomplished free-lance writer. His 400+ stories and articles have appeared over the past 30 years in *Christian Herald, Christian Standard, Sunday Digest, Young Ambassador,* and scores of other periodicals. He is also a 20-year veteran high school English teacher, specializing in such courses as creative writing, journalism, and sportswriting. To this book he brings knowledge gleaned not only as teacher and writer, but also as editor of *Boy Life,* a Sunday school weekly published by Standard Publishing Company, and as a pastor in Lancaster, Pennsylvania.

He received his education in English at Albany State Teachers College, New York (BA) and Hofstra University (MA). In addition, he has studied at Shelton College (diploma in Bible), the University of Vermont, Eastern Baptist College, Long Island University, and various summer writers' conferences.

Married and the father of two grown children, Mr. Folprecht has diverse interests, particularly sports an history.

In this book this craftsman now pulls together his b' background in education and publishing to present a tical handbook for Christian apprentice-writers.